P9-ARF-314

French Toast

Also by Harriet Welty Rochefort

French Fried

French Toast

An American in Paris Celebrates the

Maddening Mysteries of the French

Harriet Welty Rochefort

Thomas Dunne Books

St. Martin's Griffin

New York

THOMAS DUNNE BOOKS.
An imprint of St. Martin's Press.

FRENCH TOAST. Copyright © 1997, 1999, 2010 by Harriet Welty
Rochefort. All rights reserved. Printed in the United States of America.
For information, address St. Martin's Press, 175 Fifth Avenue,
New York, N.Y. 10010.

Illustration on the chapter-opening pages © 1997 by David Roth.

www.thomasdunnebooks.com
www.stmartins.com

The Library of Congress has cataloged the hardcover
edition as follows:

Rochefort, Harriet Welty.
   French toast : an American in Paris celebrates the maddening
mysteries of the French / Harriet Welty Rochefort.
     p. cm.
   ISBN 978-0-312-19978-4
   1. Rochefort, Harriet Welty—Homes and haunts—France—
Paris. 2. Paris (France)—Social life and customs—20th century—
Humor. 3. National characteristics. French—humor.
4. Americans—France—Paris—Biography. 5. Women
journalists—France—Paris—Biography. I. Title.
DC718.A44R63 1999
944'.36081—dc21

                                 98-31419
                                      CIP

ISBN 978-0-312-64278-5 (trade paperback)

First published in France by Anglophone S.A. in a somewhat different form.

D 10 9 8 7 6 5 4

To the memory of my parents, Paul and Doris Welty

Contents

Acknowledgments

French Toast owes a great debt to many people. My French family generously included me in their lives from the very beginning. Thanks to my mother-in-law, I learned how to cook a few decent meals. My sister-in-law, the epitome of French chic, taught me a lot about the Frenchwoman, which is why I use her as an example so frequently.

My American family—the late Doris Welty-Bury; Miriam Welty Trangsrud and Chuck Trangsrud; John Welty; Ward, Jane, and Ryan Welty—has always supported me in every way, beginning with my mother, who very wisely never tried to keep me at home. This book was an attempt to explain to them what it's really like to live abroad.

Many people helped with this book in different ways and I apologize to anyone I may have left out inadvertently. Bob and Ann Campbell, Sarah Colton, Dorie Denbigh, Martine Gérard, Mercedes Guerric, Richard Hill, Fred Painton, Ron and Betty Rosbottom, Nancy and Pierre Sayer, and Jan Tabet proffered pertinent, judicious, and sensitive observations. Judy Fayard unwittingly inspired this book—as European editor of the now-defunct *European Travel & Life*, she asked me to contribute articles on life in France, large parts of which appear in two of the chapters of this book. Jayne Binet, Jill Bourdais, Dr. Hiraoki Ota, and Alain Schifres graciously agreed to be interviewed. Janet Thorpe, Nancy Sayer, and Marcia Lord generously took the time to proofread the manuscript. *French Toast* owes its name to the late Lambert Mayer and his friends at Trim International and Business Wire. My gratitude to my agent, Regula Noetzli, for her efficiency, and my editor, Karyn Marcus, for her enthusiastic support.

Finally, my expert adviser and partner, Philippe Rochefort, has borne with me through thick and thin. He has grappled with my gripes, listened for hours on end to my opinions of the French school system, proofread my copy, worked the Mac (which I treat as a glorified typewriter), caught errors, and let me interview him. Without him, *French Toast* would never have seen the light of day. Nicolas, Benjamin, and David, the three Rochefort sons, were of constant inspiration and help with this project. They, too, were interviewed and helped me with their considerable computer skills, but mostly they were what they are: really fine young men and great company.

This book was definitely not written by a committee. The opinions in it are, as they say, mine and mine alone.

French Toast

Introduction

Cultural Differences—Forever Fresh

When *French Toast* was published thirteen years ago, I was both gratified and surprised by how quickly it found its niche. As one amused reader passed it on to another, it became clear that it appealed to a range of sensibilities: those interested in France, those interested in living in France, those interested in an American living in France, those interested in an American married to a Frenchman and who had two children, plus the challenge of French in-laws who didn't speak English. Although all of them got a laugh from it or even maybe learned something from entering "my world," the ones who identified the most furiously with my little tale were, understandably, like me: women who had married a Frenchman and who were living in France trying to cope with the issues of cultural adjustment which one can blithely ignore when a tourist. One of the many letters I received was from a woman who, like me, was an American married to a Frenchman and living in France. "All this time I thought that I was crazy or my husband was," she penned. "But after reading your book, I see that what I thought was sheer insanity can be chalked up to all those cultural differences. Thanks for allowing me to breathe deeper and relax."

I loved the idea of enabling this reader to "relax" and enjoy herself and not get bogged down in the craziness of life in a foreign culture. In fact the main reason I wrote the book was to explain cultural differences to myself and to try to cool down about Things the French Did That Drove Me Insane and get beyond the question of "Is my French husband nuts or is it me?" From the way the French drove and the way they colorfully insulted each other to the cold way Parisian mothers didn't greet me in front of the school to . . . well, for the rest, you can read the book. . . . At the time I wrote this, though, I was having such a hard time that there seemed to be no alternative; either I wrote down all the things I found "funny" and couldn't get used to—or I left the country before my frustration turned to hostility. Since I didn't want to leave, I decided to jot down every single aspect of French life that seemed odd, curious, or mysterious—

and the list turned into the book *French Toast*. It was a good thing for me and, I'd like to think, for some of my readers. Not only did I cool down, but I've also enjoyed life in France in a much different and fuller way than I ever expected. Yes, the French are "funny"—but so are we. . . .

Every year I'm asked to speak to groups of newly arrived Americans and Europeans who don't know what to expect in this very different country where the ways of acting and behaving seem to be so much more important than elsewhere. "Live and let live" isn't really a French thing to do. If I lived in Finland or Brazil, I doubt I'd get as many calls for help as I do in France where there's a much greater chance that someone not in the know can make a big gaffe. I shudder to think of all the ones I made early on, many of which are set in stone forever in this book.

I was far from imagining that my interest in cultural differences, an interest stemming from my very practical concern about trying to fit into French society, was shared by thousands of people, who either have come to France as tourists or who have never come at all. The reaction to *French Toast* proved to me that Americans, whether Francophiles or Francophobes, are simultaneously intrigued, intimidated, or incensed by the French. The same goes for the French who are simultaneously in admiration of, fascinated and/or repelled by the Americans.

Scores of books written by academics and journalists have tried to get to the bottom of this mutual fascination—some would say this mutual love-hate. A handful of books, such as mine, have been written by the Total Immersion people, Americans who have married French people and lived their lives in France and whose views are necessarily different because they are writing from their own experiences and not from theory.

I always think about this when my Francophile friends come to visit. Some stay a few days or a week, others, especially the ones who are professors on sabbatical leaves, for much longer. On one hand, since they don't live here all the time, they are less blasé, less jaded. They're thrilled to discover that special goat cheese they'd never seen or tasted before. They go gaga over the Paris shopping and cultural scene. They wonder why the French seem to spend so much time in cafés and why they always seem to be on strike (well, so do I). But the ones who stay around long enough find themselves alternately admiring of, mystified by, or simply ticked off by the French way. My book was an effort to figure out why. . . .

A Personal Tale

Let's face it: being married to a Frenchman and feeling the imperative need to figure things out in order to fit into his world was a powerful motivating factor. Unlike an academic grappling with arcane points of French history or philosophy at a safe intellectual remove or a tourist struggling to order from a menu, I was here for the long haul. I needed to buy groceries, needed to understand what my mother-in-law was saying to me (hoping it was nice), needed to make appointments to see the doctor and the plumber, and when I got the appointments, understand what they were saying. Not only did I need to talk to and understand these people in French—I needed to answer them in French. And when, many years later, I was able to do both of those with ease, I needed to go a step further. I needed to figure out the unspoken language, the language of nuances and codes that is so important in France. For by then I had learned that in France what is *not* said is often as important as what *is* said.

After I married, I quickly moved from the status of College Girl on a Fling in Paris to Wife of a Frenchman, complete with French in-laws. I suddenly found myself in a small Paris apartment, my dreams of a huge American house left by the roadside. I found myself racking my brains to figure out what to serve my French in-laws for dinner and made a lot of mistakes which I recount in the chapter on French food. The biggest challenge of all, though, came when we decided that our children would attend French schools. If it's the penultimate chapter in the book, it's because the French educational system had me totally stymied. I solved that one quickly: since my French husband survived it, he got to deal with it. It turned out to be the best decision I ever made. And here's a nice end to the story: my two sons survived the French system! The one who went the *prépa* and *grandes écoles* route is now a software engineer in Montreal (nicely combining the French and English speaking parts of his life). His brother, who wanted nothing to do with the *grandes écoles,* studied philosophy at the Sorbonne and has just published his first novel with the prestigious French publishing house Gallimard (think Camus, says the proud mother. . . .). And in one of those ironic twists of fate, the son I thought was my little American turned out to be TOTALLY French, and the son I thought was TOTALLY French turned out to be much more American. Fortunately, my stepson, Nicolas, a neurologist in Marseilles, is a bona fide Frenchman, so no surprises there!

Just in case anyone thinks that I'm the only one in my couple who's on the alert for cultural differences, I should add here and now that my French husband has his own personal laundry list of how the Americans are different. That would make a separate, and very entertaining book. Only one problem: for all the faults they have, the French have one quality we Americans don't. Ready? Since they live in a society where criticism, although painful, is seen as necessary and even a path to improvement, they are more inured to it. They can dish it out in spades but some of them at least are able to laugh when their foibles are pointed out, even by a foreigner—whereas I highly doubt that a book by a French person pointing out the "oddities" of Americans would be seen as anything more than Gallic arrogance (an expression, by the way, that has become a tired cliché and not *always* appropriate). Food for thought . . . and correct me if I'm wrong.

Since this is a personal tale, there are a couple of caveats. First of all, readers are advised that this is MY life and MY tale, and in no way "the truth about the French." It is my reaction to France and the French based on where I come from and who I am and where I am in France and with whom. The book would have been quite different had I been a New Yorker marrying into a rural French family, or a Southerner marrying into an artistocratic French family, or a Catholic or Jewish or Muslim American married to a French Muslim or Jew from the countryside. But that's not the case. I am a WASP (a term our politically correct language still allows), born and raised in the heartland of the United States, married to a Frenchman from a traditional Catholic family, who was born and raised in Paris with parents whose families came from the isolated mountainous Auvergne region of France and the *foie gras* land of Périgord in the southwest.

My husband was born in Paris and is very Parisian, and Parisians, like New Yorkers, are NOT like people in the provinces. They have a different way of speaking, acting, walking, talking. Like all big-city people, they're in a hurry. They can be cold and nasty but, if you get to know them, can be (almost) warm and funny. Since Paris is made up of little villages, if you stick around your *arrondissement* long enough, you'll get to know the baker, the butcher, and the *fromager*. If you're a tourist passing through, you won't see this "neighborly" aspect of the French. Speaking of French neighbors, I've had a smattering of just about everything, low to high social class (a Marquise!), rich, poor, noisy, quiet. The only thing my various neighbors had in common was their discretion. In Paris most people simply want to avoid each other (although I've heard of entire buildings in which the neighbors exchange recipes and keep each other's children—I keep HOPING I'll end up in a place like that). Note to all those who think I write from the point of view of the American who's never frequented any parts of Paris other than the Latin Quarter or the chic West of Paris, I've lived in the ritzy 16th and upscale Neuilly, the staid 7th, the intellectual 5th, the "normal" 15th, and now the working class going bourgeois bohemian 20th. *Et oui!*

And now let's go one further. I'm from Iowa. This is odd, definitely odd, *non*? Even in the States, people would ask me "how I got out." (Funny, huh? I walked out, barefoot, I tell them.)

Criticizing the French

When, as sometimes happens, the French accuse me of criticizing them (which they rarely do, since as I mentioned above, they are more used to giving and taking criticism in a culture that values it), I just repeat their own expression "*qui aime bien chatie bien*" ("the more you care about someone, the harder you are on him").

It's easy, sometimes too easy, to criticize a foreign culture, to use it as a scapegoat. BFT (Before *French Toast*) I did that a LOT. The writing of *French Toast* taught me that before automatically criticizing it's preferable to try to understand—which is what I encourage the newly arrived to do. There definitely was an AFT (After *French Toast*) in which I controlled, or at least tried to, my kneejerk reactions and finally accepted the fact of "when in Rome." Of course when some bureaucratic jerk is bawling you out or some salesperson is filing her nails instead of serving you, it's hard to stand there and tell yourself to understand. . . .

Things I Still Don't Get

In case I'm giving you the mistaken impression that writing *French Toast* cleared up all the little mysteries of French culture and that I have gently fallen into a

Pollyannish state of beatitude, let me clarify. The fact that I understand the French concept of *laïcité* doesn't mean that I understand why the French sabotage their own universities with useless strikes, why they're letting the Sorbonne go down the drain, why they want to cut your head off if you stand out, why they don't encourage their young people to stay in, not flee, France, why they tax the rich . . . and the list is long.

I still don't understand (but do admire) how the French can be so comfortable with ambiguity. We Anglos want detailed instructions and procedures. The French don't feel uneasy if there aren't any. For example, one recent weekend my husband and I traveled to Marseilles to attend the year-end concert of the dance school our little seven-year-old granddaughter is in. We were told that it was quite an event, that it would take place in a beautiful old theater in the town, so we packed a change of clothes to look decent and off we went.

When the curtain came up, everyone gasped and clapped as a line of perfectly smiling four-year-olds in pastel colored tutus began to dance. I looked at my program and saw that this was indeed the "class baby" (in English for some odd reason). I then looked around to see if anyone besides me was wondering where on earth the director or the master of ceremonies was. I couldn't fathom that no one was there to explain about the various classes, the music chosen, the dance steps, the progression of the students during the year. When I said that to my French daughter-in-law, she replied: "But there was a program."

The point is that the French are not uncomfortable, are even quite comfortable, with what they call *le flou artistique*, which could be translated as an artistic vagueness. It means that they can handle not knowing, but just enjoying what they see. An American, or at least this American, wants more structure, more framework, more information.

At the end of the performance a woman I presumed was the director stepped on stage. I presumed this because she was offered flowers and she then clapped her hands to applaud the performance of her students. At least, I think that's what it was. I'll never know. (And, hey, is it really that important?!)

Changes

A lot of changes have come about since I wrote this book. As I said, I changed after writing it simply because investigating topics that disturbed me dramatically de-dramatized them. For example, I thought that all kinds of truly horrid things were happening in my kids' classes at school because we parents were not exactly welcomed (see chapter on education) but when I actually got inside a classroom, I was impressed by all the good work going on in there.

Almost all of the material in the book is timeless and I see in rereading it, that if I were to turn the clock back, essentially I'd write the exact same book. Some things that have changed since its writing are that France has gone nonsmoking so I could no longer riff on second-hand smoke, and French parents, after making fun of Americans for their laxity in child-raising, have gone the Dr. Spock way. French children can be as bratty as American children! As far as the strictness in schools that I described in the chapter on education, it still exists in some places—but there's more and more violence in schools (with knives, not guns, since this is France with strict gun laws) and less respect for teachers. The world changed as well. With 9/11 came a lot of hate mail from many Americans who couldn't understand why the French wouldn't side with Bush on Iraq. Things heated up in France as well. Most, not all, of the French were against Bush and against the war in Iraq but didn't take out their disagreement on Americans *personally*. An American journalist friend of mine was asked by the editor of a major U.S. news operation to do in-the-street interviews with Americans who, he was convinced, were being chastized and raked over the coals by the French. When she reported back that there was no "news" on that front, that the Americans she interviewed were pleasantly surprised that there were no tensions, he was incredulous and disappointed. That underscores another cultural difference: France is an old country which has had many wars leading to dissension among friends and within families. The French are used to debate and dis-agreement and capable of being in total disaccord with friends but keeping the friendship—once again, it's that quality of being comfortable with ambiguity, the gray area.

But Bush and the Iraq war did indeed give the French a perfect excuse to unleash a latent, generalized anti-Americanism that I had never seen before Bush, and did it ever come out. From the death penalty to the right to own guns, the French were all over us. They were right, we were wrong! (OK, all right already, but did they have to rub it in? Ouch!) And, just as quickly, when Obama won the supreme victory, we found ourselves back in favor. That was nice—I can quit saying I'm Canadian. . . .

The Sarkozy Years

Another factor of change since I wrote this book was the election of Nicolas Sarkozy to the presidency of France. The proof that it's easier to write about sex than money since the French have fewer complexes about the first than the second has been proved a thousand times over by the ebullient, iconoclastic Sarkozy. His Ray Bans and Rolexes and yacht trips shook up the French much more than the coming out of President François Mitter-rand's secret love child and the view of Mitterrand's two families—the wife and the mistress—standing together at attention at his funeral. French president Félix Faure died in the arms of his mistress, but the sexual peccadilloes of former French presidents were nothing compared to the way Sarkozy played hard and fast with his money in his *nouveau riche* way. In a country where wealth is best hidden, his ostentation was unseemly, even shocking. Added to that was his breaking the unspoken pact by which French presidents kept their families in the background and their mistresses off in a corner. Sarkozy very publicly divorced and remarried in office and—who knows—perhaps he'll be the first President to father a child while in office as well.

So, French or American?

French people, upon hearing my accent (hard not to), often ask me which country I like best, France or America. Americans who know I've lived in France longer than I've lived in the States ask me if I've "gone native," become French. To me, the answer is clear: Although I have a French passport and French citizenship and a deep affection for my adopted country, I'm as American as apple pie, as my five ancestors who fought in the Revolutionary War, as the Fourth of July, the day I'm writing this introduction, and as Thanksgiving, my favorite American holiday, which I celebrate every year in

France (French turkeys, by the way, are delicious and take half as long to bake!). I must admit I never read much of Gertrude Stein or liked what I read but I know and totally identify with her famous phrase, a phrase that provides a perfect answer to all those questions about whether I've gone native or which country I prefer: "America is my country and Paris is my hometown."

Vive la France! Vive l'Amérique!

Paris, July 4, 2009

The French Connection

I arrived in France not just from the United States but from Shenandoah, a small town in Iowa. Tucked into the southwest corner of the state, near the borders of Missouri and Nebraska, Shenandoah was the center of my life until I was twenty years old. And small-town life in the Midwest has forever conditioned my reactions to what came after. Coming from Iowa, rather than New York or California, put a different spin on my experience. An example: Growing up in a small town in the Midwest, I just assumed that everyone in the entire world was friendly and straight-shooting. *Quelle surprise!* (What a surprise!)

French Toast grew out of two decades of living in France with a French husband, a full-scale French family-in-law, two half-French, half-American children, and a French stepson. Rather than just gently fading into French culture—that is, adapting—I have come to realize I feel more and more American. Increasingly, I find myself trying to explain to myself why the French are the way they are, and why, in spite of "going native" in the sense of having a French spouse, speaking the language fluently, and immensely enjoying living here, I don't feel any more French than the day I arrived. This book stemmed from a desire to write it all down. In addition to being a cathartic experience for its author, *French Toast* will, I hope, be informative and enjoyable for each reader while providing a few keys to the complex character of the French.

As an Iowan freelance journalist residing in France, I have had a bird's-eye view of the French for these past twenty years.

Sitting astride this French-American fence has given me a privileged position of being both participant and observer. Being neither fish nor fowl has given me a constant comparative view of both life in the United States and life in France, as well as perceptions about the French that tourists rarely acquire. For example, life with the French has put a whole new meaning on the word *complicated*. The simplest situation in France suddenly becomes something extremely complex and detailed. The French attention to detail—from the way one cuts cheese to the color of one's panty hose—has never ceased to fascinate me.

Based on common and daily experiences, *French Toast* is a mixture of reflections and observations about life in France. These include all the *faux-pas* I have made in the past and continue to make (laughing too loudly, saying things directly instead of obliquely, cutting my lettuce leaves instead of folding them, just to mention a few examples).

More than anything else, I think this book reflects a whole range of different emotions—affection, wonder, and, sometimes, plain exasperation. I can't relate to the way the French drive (although my American friends tell me I drive like a real Parisian and are they ever scared), but I would *much* rather get into a political discussion with the French than with my compatriots, because the French basically have mastered the art of arguing politely without getting unpleasantly personal. As one recently arrived American remarked, "You can get into a violent political discussion, which is followed by a big laugh and 'Please pass the cheese,' and you go on to something else."

Come to think about it, it may seem contradictory, but I feel rather more at home sometimes with the French because of their refreshing lack of what they call *"le puritanisme."* On the other hand, the minute I set foot back in the States, the tension I feel while living in Paris eases out of me as I enjoy the civility of people who aren't afraid to be nice to one another even if their families haven't known one another for the past two hundred years.

In sum, I took off my rose-colored glasses a long time ago. The illusions I came with—and there were plenty—have been replaced by a rather fond and amazed look at the French (including my own children, who are so French sometimes that I can hardly believe they are my own). What follows is not a sociological study of the French, but a straightforward and personal tale of what makes the French so French.

Meet Philippe

During this book, I interview Philippe, my French husband, to counterbalance my typically American point of view on the French. He deserves this opportunity. After all, he's put up with my comments for the past twenty years, so it's only fair to give him a chance to say what he thinks about what I think.

So who is Philippe, and is he typically French?

Although he was born and raised in the fifteenth arrondissement of Paris, Philippe's parents hailed from the south of France, the imposing mountains of the Auvergne and the softer scenery of the Dordogne. In spite of these rural roots, he is a "real" Parisian, having attended French public schools and then attending two years of *prépa* before going to a *grande école* (see the chapter on education to figure this out). Along the way, he also picked up a doctoral degree in economics. Extracurricular activities included playing his guitar in cafés and bass with a jazz group. Summers were spent on holidays in Spain, where he picked up Spanish, and trips to England, where he learned English with an English accent (which he had when I met him, but over the years it has been transformed into a more American accent). He has an uncanny talent for picking up accents and has been known to fool both Japanese and Arabs when speaking the one or two sentences he knows in each of these languages.

Philippe loves history, in particular the Middle Ages, and historical monuments. He loves to cook and is a hospitable host. He likes to read, play the piano and guitar, and paint in oils. He hates cars and the consumer society. He's not all that hot for sports (either participating or observing). He likes our cat, and, believe me, not many people do. He likes America and Americans (hey, he married me, didn't he?). Some people say he looks like former French president Jacques Chirac—an observation he is not so sure he likes.

Considering that there are Frenchmen who hate history, can't stand reading, love cars, the consumer society, and sports, and are anti-American, can we say that Philippe is typically French? Let's just say that he is very French and you'd have a hard time mistaking him for any other nationality. To begin with, he has a typical Parisian expression on his face—that is, Don't mess with me, baby (which is great, because he scares the daylights out of panhandlers and all those people I have trouble fending off due to my big, naïve, ever-present smile). Second, he has a slight tendency to explode, only to calm down just as quickly. Third, he can carry on a conversation concerning just about anything, and fourth, he is very polite in that mysteriously hard-to-define and often inscrutable French way. Finally, like many Frenchmen, he can be France's best critic. Deep in his heart, though, you know he couldn't live anywhere else. He's simply too French.

Getting Here

When you grow up in a small town in the southwest corner of Iowa, probably the most exotic thing you could possibly think of would be France. That is, of course, if you were of the bent to think of exotic places and people. And I was.

As a youngster, I loved my family and friends, had no particular yearnings for anything other than what I had. What did I have? A warm, safe, loving environment far from the pressures, stress, and aspirations of city life (we didn't even know what or where the prestigious eastern colleges were, let alone aspire to go to them). At the same time, I was fully convinced that destiny was going to tap me on the shoulder and *I was going to get out of there* and go a long way away. That I knew.

I remember standing at the top of the stairs of our beautiful Victorian house and hearing a knock at the door. I was convinced that it was someone who had come for me, someone who knew that I should be somewhere else, someone who would whisk me away to a strange and foreign land. My heart quickened at the thought. It was only the mailman—and he didn't even have anything for me!

But I continued to *know* that I would end up somewhere exotic. A banal existence was not for me, child of the cornfields. (Well, not really, although both sides of my family had been in farming forever; my father and one of his brothers were the first to go to "town," so I didn't grow up in the country. Still, my grandparents and uncles all farmed the land around us.)

The special thing that finally happened was that, after the death of my paternal grandmother, my grandfather remarried a woman who was a professor of French at Grinnell College. She was to have a capital influence on my life, telling me all about France, where she had lived for a time, even marrying a Frenchman, whom she eventually divorced. She brought me books about France, taught me French words. With her beautiful white hair and blue eyes and the breath of foreign air she brought with her, she totally won me over. From age eight, I knew I had to go to France, if only to have a look and come right back home.

After college, when everyone else was headed toward jobs or marriage, I headed straight to France. Actually, I hopped on a boat in San Francisco, jumped off in Acapulco, got back on a freighter in Veracruz and traveled to ports in South America, the Canary Islands, and Spain before hitting my final destination.

I *loved* Paris. It was all my stepgrandmother had told me, and more. The first night I was in Paris, I boarded a *bateau-mouche* to cruise down the Seine; the air was soft and warm, a man spoke some unintelligible words to me in French, and I was conquered—by the sound of the language, the way people walked and moved, even the air, which seemed different. I felt I had walked into a Toulouse-Lautrec painting. Later, I would find Paris too noisy, too traffic-filled. But that first heady moment was a strong one. I felt I should savor that moment, leave Paris in my mind as a beautiful memory, and head for a new destination—South America. I was on my way when I met Philippe.

It's not that he swept me off my feet. In fact, when I saw him, I thought that in my entire life I had never seen anyone with such a scowl on his face. In spite of his expression, though, he had one of the driest, funniest senses of humor I had ever encountered. This very typical, totally chauvinistic (he denies this charge) Frenchman became very good company. And then we married.

As my husband periodically points out, I chose to come to France, and to stay. I did not arrive kicking and screaming, someone's bride, wrested from her native land. I came of my own free will and am free to leave anytime I decide I don't like this place anymore (he says this on days when I am making critical noises about my adopted land). True, but it's not so easy. Wherever you live becomes your home, whether you like some of it, all of it, or not much of it. My home is here and I love living in France, but that doesn't mean that my thoughts about the French are not ambiguous. The cultural gaps, which seemed small twenty years ago, grow larger, not smaller, with time. When you've signed on for the long haul, you start to have a definite opinion on matters you didn't really care all that much about and didn't have to deal with initially (in my case, the French family, education, attitudes). You are both appreciative and critical of the host culture in a way you wouldn't be if you had remained safely at home. Even the word *home* takes on a different meaning. Once when I spoke of "home," I was referring to the United States. Now, I realize "home" is where I live—that is, France.

As far as I can see, American couples living in France have a very different perception of France and the French. France is an interlude in their lives, but they retain their Americanness as a couple. They are a united front. The adjustments they make to the culture are the ones they wish to make, not ones they have to make.

With a Franco-American couple, on the other hand, there is always a push and pull—over what language to speak, over what schools to put your kids in, over what religious instruction to give them, if any. Over attitudes. I call the French negative, weighed down by history. My husband says Americans are positive to the point of being naïve because, *justement*, they have no sense of history.

My first reaction to anything new is always "Fantastic!" My husband's is "Why change?" We meet a new couple and I say, "Aren't they nice?" And my husband will say, "They're rather nice" *(assez gentils)*, which means that if he could get to know them over the next two hundred years, he'd have the time to judge.

I am overwhelmingly enthusiastic, my husband less so. I don't suspect everyone I meet of having ulterior motives; my husband is always on his guard. And so on. This doesn't mean he's not a great guy, but we find we do have different viewpoints. Fortunately, we have moved beyond the point of taking sides on who is "right" and who is "wrong." We just chalk up a lot of misunderstandings to cultural differences.

You come here and you think that (apart from a few details) France is more similar to the United States than many other countries. After all, you could have gone to China or Japan. But in truth, living in France is almost as different as living in China or Japan. Because as the years go by, you, the American *immigrée,* discover that cultural differences run deep below the surface and that what once appeared to be minor quirks are actually major differences.

French Toast is the story of what those cultural gaps turned out to be.

The French and Their Food

The most awesome experiences in France revolve around cuisine. It's one thing to partake of wonderful French food prepared by eminent chefs in four-star restaurants and quite another to turn out full-fledged French meals in your own home twice a day. Fortunately for me, my husband's mother, sister, and aunt are all wonderful cooks and hostesses and generous with their knowledge.

Catching on to French food was both easy and complicated. Easy because I had excellent teachers right in my husband's family. Complicated because, well, deep in my mental pantry, I have a hard time trying to think of what to serve for two full-scale four- to five-course meals a day, seven days a week.

My French sister-in-law doesn't seem to have this

problem. In the family country house, where there are always at least ten people at the table, I watch with wonder as she casually composes each meal. "Now what shall we have for lunch?" she'll query, thinking of all the possibilities and combinations. And before I have the time to say, "Nothing," which for my French in-laws would be unthinkable in any event, or "Every man for himself," which would also be out of the question, she has come up with an answer. Or a possible answer: Her final choice will depend on what looks good at the market that day.

An example might be pâté to start with, then *magret de canard* (breast of duck) cut into little fillets, accompanied by fresh peas and new potatoes, followed by a big green salad with a delicious homemade vinaigrette, and finally a big plate of wonderful cheese (Brie, Camembert, a chèvre, a blue d'Auvergne) and then ice cream, cake, or fruit, depending on what went before.

I could report that my sister-in-law goes to this trouble only on weekends, but it's not true. What I just described was a Saturday noon meal. On Saturday night, she proposed a different menu, composed of fresh asparagus with a sauce mousseline, a potato omelette (a family specialty) accompanied by a beautiful lettuce (real lettuce, not iceberg) salad, cheese (again), and a *tarte aux fraises* (strawberry pie). Whatever the spread is, my sister-in-law is afraid we aren't getting enough to eat. What?!

I am in awe not just of how effortlessly she pulls all this off but also of one thing that has never ceased to intrigue me: SHE NEVER WEARS AN APRON. Not only am I incapable of dreaming up daily menus like hers (but I'm improving, maybe in another twenty years?); I can't get *near* a kitchen without staining my clothes. My perfectly manicured and made-up French sister-in-law stands around in a silk blouse and high-heeled shoes as grease spatters about her but never comes within a centimeter of her.

As an American in a French family, I quickly caught on to the system of courses: the first, the main, the salad, the cheese, the dessert, all of which follow one another and aren't served together. Being an American with a sweet tooth, thinking of what to serve for dessert never posed a problem for me. I also adore the cheese course because it's sheer pleasure to select what you want out of the tremendous variety available—the more pungent, the better. The winner on the odor score is the *Boulette d'Avesnes*, a beer-based *vache* (cow cheese) rolled in a red pepper dust. If you can swallow a hunk of this stuff, you can down anything cheesy in France. Philippe perversely loves to bring home a *Boulette*, especially when we're expecting guests. It's a test of character. Remember de Gaulle, who asked rhetorically, "How can anyone govern a country with four hundred and fifty different cheeses?" That may not be the number, but the point is that there are so many kinds, the number changes every time the story is told.

The best thing about both the dessert and the cheese is that you can go buy them—good-bye homemade hassle. (You can also buy the pâté; no one in his right mind would *make* one unless that person had several hours to kill.) When it comes to actually *concocting* food à la Harriet, well, over the years (thanks to my mother-in-law and my husband's aunt), I managed to get a few main dishes down pat. In fact, I even got to be rather good or, as the French would say, *pas mal* ("not bad") at *plats mijotés*, those slow-simmering dishes that cook for hours and taste good even a day or two later. When I go to the market and find a cut of meat I don't recognize or a fish whose name means nothing to me, I just ask the *marchand* what it is and how to make it (the result is generally a new recipe), and believe me, these guys know what they're talking about when it comes to food. *Et voilà!*

The killer for me was, and still is, the hors d'oeuvre. Anyway, why have one? "Why don't we just move to the essential?" I asked my husband. "Because," he replied, "if you start with something, even if it's just a little something, you won't be as tempted to eat so much of what is to come." Not bad reasoning, I thought. So I have made a bit of an effort but have yet to live up to my in-laws' standards. Their first course is so copious that in the beginning, I thought it *was* the meal. A few bellyaches later, I realized you've got to go easy on the first course if you want to make it to the end of the meal without losing face, or anything else.

None of the above knowledge came easily, but that's okay, because as an American living in France, I can take refuge in the fact that they (the French in general and my French family in particular) have some five centuries of food culture behind them and I have only a couple. So it stands to reason that just *thinking* about all this is an effort for me and as natural as breathing for them.

When I first came to France over twenty years ago, I decided to introduce the concept of The Sandwich As A Meal to my in-laws. This was pre-McDonald's, when people like my father-in-law still returned home for lunch, a four-course affair. My mother-in-law, used to the preparation of two ample daily repasts, embraced my idea eagerly. We hence proceeded to prepare sandwiches for lunch and serve one to my father-in-law, normally the soul of tolerance. He gazed at our creation as if it were a strange living creature and, upon being informed that you ate The Sandwich with your hands, commented ironically, "Well, why don't we all just get down on the floor and throw bones over our shoulders while we're at it?" That, needless to say, was the last time we ever even entertained the idea of fast food in that family. My father-in-law has since died, but tradition holds. In my *belle-famille*, a sandwich is not a meal.

In spite of their marvelous culinary tradition, the French seem to be turning up their collective noses at fast food less and less (unfortunately). But not *all* the French. My mother-in-law and sister-in-law wouldn't know what "a McDo," the French nickname for the hamburger emanating from Ray Kroc's ubiquitous chain, looked like if it was plopped down in front of them, and I have a hard time imagining either of them serving sandwiches for the midday meal or getting their impeccably manicured fingers around sliced bread. They're having too much fun doing "real" food.

There's another reason for leaving the kitchen to my French family. My mother-in-law in particular (but my husband, too) has *manies* (obsessions), mostly concerning vegetables. For example, washing salads. In my family, my husband has washed lettuce leaves for the past twenty years. This was after he discovered that I hadn't mastered the technique and probably never would. The technique is separating the leaves one by one and looking at every single leaf to make sure it is perfectly clean and void of those little fleas that prove the lettuce came from a field, then washing the good ones and ripping (not cutting) each leaf one by one into just the right size.

My husband flips out at the sight of an imperfect leaf of lettuce, so, hey, he gets to clean them!

Then there are carrots: You cut out the pithy green inside. Tomatoes: My mother-in-law peels them and gently squeezes out the seeds when preparing a tomato salad. (When I do this, it looks like an ax murder. Her salad is a perfect jewel.) Roasts: Slices have to be thin, never thick. My husband, bless his artistic French heart, would never let a boiled *potato* out of the kitchen unless it had a bit of parsley sprinkled on it. Color! Oh yes, and if you serve a baked potato to my husband or any other Frenchman, he will cheerfully remove every single bit of skin before attacking it. "Only hogs eat potato skins," exclaims my husband, watching me in horror as I eat the potato, *peau* and all.

Now, in all truth, I *do* actually put on two meals a day, but I am the first to confess that my husband is the one who has the talent and the ideas. In this, he is an exception. I don't know a lot of other Frenchmen who are so gifted in the kitchen. His *blanquette de veau* is to die for. His potato omelette is perfect. He also makes crêpes. (I can make them, but he can both make them and flip them just so.) Whatever he rustles up is simply delicious. And he does it all with that perfect French nonchalance. I admit I am just a teeny bit vexed when, after years of valiant efforts of thinking up menus and making major meals, people say, "Oh, Philippe is such a wonderful cook!" I shouldn't be, though, because he's also the soul of hospitality and has what we laughingly refer to as the *"syndrome du chef"*—that is, he *likes* to feed people! In fact, I should thank my lucky stars that when guests come, he often does the whole deal and I get so relaxed, I think I'm at someone else's party.

Things are *much* better, though, than they once were. A year after I got married, I decided to take the plunge and invite French guests to dinner. Like a general going into battle, I planned my attack. My strategy was to think out the meal from back to front—that is, retreating from the dessert course methodically back through to the starter (which probably violates all principles of gastronomy, but that's okay). Nerves are nerves, and my first attempt was fraught with errors. My first course was a simple lettuce salad with chicken livers and bacon tossed with a vinaigrette. I didn't consider that not everyone likes chicken livers and some people even hate them. So much for the hors d'oeuvre. I tried not to look crushed as the guests pushed those tender bits to the edges of their plates. I thought the French loved liver!

As for the chicken and rice, I mean, how can you go astray when you serve something as basic as a roast chicken? You can in France. One of my guests, a French friend, kindly requested the sauce, which, in the heat of the moment, I had forgotten to serve. Then there was the cheese course. Since the cheese had been stinking up the kitchen, I had put it in the fridge and had forgotten to take it out. So when it arrived at the table, it was cold

and had congealed—a major booboo at the French table.
The crème caramel of course didn't have enough caramel. To top it all off, I hadn't realized how much bread
French guests can consume, and I'd had to escape in my
apron to the local *boulangerie* just before the cheese
course. The evening lurched from one catastrophe to
another, until I was convinced that I would never, never
entertain again.

I did, of course, and elaborated the Rochefort Rule:
To save an evening, serve plenty of wine. If the guests
are relaxed enough, they won't notice the minor errors.
I mastered the major challenges: Don't forget the bread,
follow the order of courses, don't put the cheese in
the fridge, and don't serve anything on the list of no-no
foods, such as squid, oysters, and, yes, even snails or
offal. Before I knew this, I prepared a meal with squid—
yummy, yummy—and one of my guests almost threw
up before asking if she could please have some ham. So
much for squid, unless, of course, you poll your guests
before dinner: "Do you eat squid, intestines of pigs, et
cetera?" My husband and I eat all these disgusting animal parts—brains, ears, tongues, feet, you name it, so
I have to remind myself that many people, even French
ones, find them revolting.

Of course, I wouldn't make nearly as many mistakes
now as I made then, either in terms of food or social
codes. In the early days of my marriage, my husband's
boss called unexpectedly from the airport to inform us

that he was in town. I would have let it go by saying, "great, nice to talk to you," but my husband interpreted the underlying meaning of the call for my innocent foreign ears. This was not a casual hello. It meant, COME AND GET ME AT THE AIRPORT AND INVITE ME TO DINNER. Not being a good French housewife, I had literally next to nothing on hand. We had also just moved into our house, and barely had any furniture, let alone any foie gras. The boss ended up perched at my kitchen table in front of an improvised omelette. There was no bread (the bakery had long since closed), no cheese, and no salad, although there was a terrible dessert. The wine was not up to par. He hated the whole experience.

This disaster did, however, teach me that it is indispensable to have decent food on hand at all times. Unfortunately, to have food, you have to shop, and to shop for staples, you have to go to the supermarket, which is way down the line of relaxing experiences one can have in France. Every time I grocery-shop in this country, which is once a week on the average, I get an acute case of the supermarket blues. In the store, you are jostled, shoved, hit from behind, and squished. It's normal: If you can fit France into Texas—and France has roughly seven times more people—it's logical that there are more people and less space in the supermarket.

I thought I was alone in my dislike of the supermarket, but after polling my friends, I found I had a lot of company. "It makes me break out in hives just to think about the weekly shopping expedition," one friend told me. Outdoor markets are much more fun and I go to them often—but when shopping for a family, one is condemned to paying regular visits to the supermarket for the basics.

The general complaint: There's no one to bag the stuff! So the whole scene looks like Charlie Chaplin in *Modern Times* with the reel speeding up and speeding up until everything falls apart. First, you are on one end of the line, getting out all your yogurt, milk, soap, and so on, then the checkout person is passing it through, and then, even before you've finished unloading the cart, you are suddenly on the other end of the counter, desperately stuffing it into flimsy tiny plastic bags.

In your haste, you see a shadow, a line of fidgety people behind you who watch as you stuff and stuff and can't quite get everything in. You still have to get in the lettuce and Q-tips and Pampers and figure out how you will get all this to the car without breaking the eggs, when you realize that the person at the cash register has finished checking it through and you have to pay.

As I bag in a frenzy, I suddenly have a vision of my mom's supermarket (Lund's in Minneapolis). As befits a northern climate, the percolator is always filled with fresh coffee, which people can sip as they shop. The aisles are wide; it is calm. A kid bags the groceries and takes them out to your car. Am I dreaming?

No wonder Parisian women look like they're in a

bad mood when they're shopping for groceries. (I say Parisian, because in the provinces, where life is slower, shopping in the supermarket can almost be a pleasure— it all depends on where you are.)

Now, let's move on to a few helpful hints on what to do when you're invited to dinner in a French home. Of course, much depends on what kind of French home (uptight or casual). When in doubt, be formal!

Other than learning that you should always have food, and preferably some fancy food, in your house, I learned that when invited, it's not always good to help out in the kitchen (I'm not much for being in the kitchen when I can be elsewhere, so this problem doesn't frequently arise for me). However, I did once trek back to the kitchen with a French friend and, to her horror, dumped what I thought was a bowl of water into the sink. It turned out that it was the syrup for her fruit salad. And she did not see the humor of the situation. So much for helping in the kitchen. Fortunately, most French dinner parties are as ritualistic as theater performances: The hostess is the star, and you're not supposed to mess up her act. This keeps people like me out of the kitchen. (More helpful hints on how to act at a dinner party will appear in the chapter on politesse: Stay tuned!)

I thought that with the importance the French attach to food and with the example of good eating habits and good food given them by their French families, my sons would grow up to teach me a thing or two about *la bouffe*. Wrong.

My French stepson is just fine on this score, as he was raised in a traditional French family. He's got a pretty ferocious appetite but eats only at meals. These French-American kids of mine, however, are a total disaster in terms of food (by French standards, that is). Why? The elder one was born with anti-French food taste buds and anti-French eating habits: He does not eat asparagus, any kind of tripe, snails, oysters, barely touches vegetables, and the only fruits he will consent to eat are bananas. He *adores* hamburgers, pizza, Coke, all that good American stuff. His idea of paradise would be to dispense with the French mealtimes and stuff himself with McDos. (Now that he is at college, that's exactly what he does, and his French friends are the ones who are astonished at his very un-French way of eating.) My younger son is not a total disaster. In fact, he will taste everything. So what's the problem? The problem is that he is capable of filling up on two full-course French meals a day, then loading up on Coke and cookies in between.

Now, this may not seem a major crime for an adolescent, but in my husband's family, it is. My mother-in-law is absolutely horrified to see her two half-French, half-American grandsons guzzling Coke. When on one occasion I asked my sister-in-law what lessons she hoped would remain with her daughters, she promptly answered, "Good eating habits and NO FAST FOOD." How disappointed they must be when they look at their grandsons and nephews. Oh well . . .

Anyway, there's hope for my two. One day, I heard the elder talking to the younger: "You know," he told him, "when I was in the United States, I had to *ask* if I could have lunch. They were going to skip it! Can you imagine?" The younger nodded his head, commiserating over the American side of his culinary culture.

So I tell myself that at least they've been exposed to good food and good eating habits in a country where this is no laughing matter. And how funny it will be for them to look back to the days when it was their French papa who made them their favorite foods—*frites* and crêpes—while their American mother harangued them about developing good French eating habits.

Food Tips from My French Mother-in-law

I have been known to call Marie-Jeanne, my mother-in-law, from vacation spots to find out how she does this or that. The last call was from Chamonix. The question was: "What cut of beef do you use for *boeuf aux carottes* and how long do you cook it?" Answer: "*Macreuse* or *jumeau,* and don't forget the *pied de veau* [veal foot, for those of you who need a translation]. Cook for a couple of hours at least at low heat." I feel fortunate in having an interactive mother-in-law who can replace a cookbook! (Time out for a confession here: I don't even know what *macreuse* or *jumeau* is other than that it's good! I often buy cuts of meat or fish which I know only by the French name. *C'est la vie.*)

- Always put something green on something white. Example: potatoes and parsley, fish and parsley. In fact, parsley can be a saving grace.
- Memorize the recipe for simple, never-fail vinaigrette: one teaspoon of mustard, one tablespoon of vinegar, three tablespoons of oil, salt, pepper, and tarragon (optional). For more quantity, just double or triple the ingredients. (Actually, she never measures, but this is about what it comes out to.) Also, the difference between a great vinaigrette and a so-so one is in the ingredients—only the best. And remember to beat in the oil gradually at the end; otherwise, your vinaigrette will not hold together.

- You can't live in France if you are unable to make your own crème caramel: My mother-in-law's crème caramel is so perfect that after one try, I gave up and decided just to enjoy eating hers. I hope someday to reproduce it by osmosis. Anyway, she tells me that the basic recipe is easy. The trick is the caramel, which should be abundant and dark brown, but not burned.
- To be accepted in the family, learn the secrets of the Rochefort potato omelette: The key is in the potatoes. Buy the kind that won't disintegrate. Peel, cut in slices, wash, and dry with a clean cloth. Fry the potatoes very slowly with goose fat. Cover until tender. Add the eggs, which have been beaten with salt and pepper and a clove of garlic which you then take out. Put something green on it (parsley). Serve the omelette with a well-seasoned green salad and plenty of red wine. Yum. Note: The trick of this simple recipe is getting the omelette onto a large serving plate without it (A) falling on the counter or floor, or (B) turning into a mess of scrambled eggs. Much practice is recommended.

A Brief Interview with Philippe

HARRIET: *Have you noticed any difference in your eating habits since you married me?*

PHILIPPE: *Yes, I'm cooking a lot more.*

The Frenchwoman

Attitudes toward sex in France are very different from those in the
United States, and in a nutshell, less puritanical. Much of the
reason for this is that Frenchwomen are far more comprehending
and tolerant of men than their American sisters. In fact,
Frenchwomen are *very* different from American women,
a fact I was to discover and eventually appreciate.

Frenchwomen were another thing I had to master. One
wouldn't think there would be much of a gap between a
woman from one Western country and a woman from
another, but there is.

Actually, I get along quite well with Frenchwomen,
outside of Paris. But the Parisian woman can be a bit
tough to take. The worst *Parisiennes* are to be found in

upper-class neighborhoods. These slim, elegantly coiffed and made-up creatures can really make you feel as if you just got off the boat, third-class, from Yemen. Even the salesladies in these neighborhoods start to get that way. I once went into a bakery and asked for the *miettes*, or crumbs, of candied chestnuts, which are less expensive than the whole candied chestnut. The saleslady looked at me with utter scorn: "We only sell whole chestnuts," she replied imperiously.

I slunk out, feeling like someone's help. But that was many years ago. Now I would yell, *"Don't you ever speak to me in that tone of voice."* Alas, I was not brave enough then.

My very first experience with Parisian coldness was with an exgirlfriend of my husband's. Being a rather friendly type, I stuck out my hand to shake hers. She looked at it as if it were a dead rat. I withdrew my outstretched hand and shoved it into my pocket.

I must admit this didn't get me off to a good start. Okay, she was an ex-girlfriend and maybe had some scores to settle. But then, her refusal to shake my hand may just have been the famous French reserve. An American working at a French magazine told me that she worked in the place a full year and a half before she began to get slightly friendly with the women there. She said that in the end, she even began to come to appreciate their distance.

Still, who wants to wait years and years to have a friend?

Once you get your French friend, you may find yourself in a different relationship than with your American friends. Perhaps because it takes so long, when it finally happens, you find yourself bound up in a very possessive kind of relationship. Your French girlfriend will tell you if your hose are the wrong color or if she doesn't like your hair or your furnishings. She can, because you are now Friends.

La Parisienne has many talents, among them giving virtuoso performances, particularly when it comes to dinner parties. Many years ago, I told my husband that I thought it would be much less of a production just to have people over for a drink. He explained to me that this wasn't done, mainly because you don't have people cross all of Paris for a drink. Therefore, if you live in Paris, you will find it almost impossible to escape the dinner party. So there you are in a Parisian home. The hostess is invariably not only slim and well coiffed, with perfect nails, but she also has done an unbeatable job of preparing the meal.

Meanwhile, the poor American slob (me) is ruminating, Why is she so perfect? Is there a secret? Why do I let it all hang out? Look at that glass of wine. I guzzle it; she sips it. *Différence*. I look at the *mousse au chocolat* and put on five pounds; she eats everything on the plate right down to the petits fours and is as slim as a rail. Oh Lord, give me a *fat* Frenchwoman. (Incidentally, large sizes in France start at a size twelve, which gives one an idea of what one is up against.)

For all of those out there who are wondering how Frenchwomen manage to stay slim in a country where food is an ongoing passion, I am here to tell you that I have found the answer! Through careful observation, I have noted that when invited to dinner parties, French-women joyfully accept everything but take minuscule portions. Many opt for a glass of fruit juice or a nonal-coholic beverage before the meal, and while they may munch on a peanut or take an olive, I have found that I generally end up taking all my before-dinner snacks back to the kitchen almost untouched.

Let me give you an example, something that oc-curred, once again, at my sister-in-law's home (the best place in town). For a little spread for ten guests, she had made marinated green, red, and yellow peppers, salmon with dill, and an aspic with foie gras and artichokes for the first course. This was followed by a *gigot d'agneau* (leg of lamb) with *pommes sarladaises* and *tomates pro-vençales*, then a cheese plate with eight different vari-eties of cheese, and, last but not least, a *mousse au chocolat*, a *tarte aux myrtilles* (blueberry pie), and a *crème caramel*. I checked out my neighbor's plate and saw that she had taken a tiny slice of the lamb with a teeny helping of potatoes. No wonder she wears a size eight dress! I checked out the plates of the other women present and can report that it was the same deal. So

although there were many delicious courses, no one
ended up feeling too full. I can also report that the
women drank champagne and red and white wine, but,
once again, in moderation. Incidentally, while we're on
the subject, it is very impolite for a woman to serve herself wine. If the glass is empty, you just have to wait for
it to be refilled. I blush to think that in my younger, innocent days, I served myself once the glass was empty.
How utterly gauche!

Then there's The Laugh: Frenchwomen emit a little
light tinkle, like pleasant bells. I (and some of my American friends) have been known to snort, snuffle, gurgle—
in short, make all kinds of noises that stridently break
ice. This is not my paranoia. A French girlfriend once
confessed to me that she was so embarrassed by the
hysterical laughter of two of her American friends that
whenever she invited them to her apartment, she made
sure to close the windows.

For some reason, Frenchwomen know how to keep
their voices down. My personal noise level is so high in
comparison that at dinner parties, I often have the feeling the sounds coming out of my mouth will shatter the
Baccarat.

Of course, Frenchwomen have a long tradition of being told to keep the decibels down. In the late nineteenth
century, the Baronne Staffe wrote, "Those who are
blessed with a soft voice have received a great gift of nature. If you are born with a soft voice, keep it therefore

like the apple of your eye; if you have received at birth a harsh voice, try to soften it. One must unceasingly keep watch over one's voice, constantly keep it at the right level. . . ."

At a rather chic party, a young boy reared up from *under* a table, where he shouldn't have been in the first place, at an inopportune moment and crashed into a tray with twelve gorgeous crystal glasses. Shards of shattered glass flew everywhere, but the hostess didn't miss a beat, busying herself with cleaning up the mess. You never would have known from looking at her perfectly composed smiling face that she was upset. Personally, I would have let out a loud scream.

Nothing has changed since Henry James wrote one hundred years ago that "French women are very formidable. In France one must count with the women."

I'd almost have a complex if I hadn't seen how positively unsisterly Frenchwomen can be. They do not band together as we do in the States. And they don't share tips. In the States, if someone you like compliments you on a new blouse, you might just tell her that you got it on sale at Saks and that if she rushes, she might be in time to get one, too. In France, this kind of sisterly sharing is something I have rarely encountered.

One Frenchwoman attempted to explain the difference between Frenchwomen and American women to me, and it made a lot of sense: "I can't see a film like *Thelma and Louise* being made in France," she stated.

"In France, we position ourselves in relation to men. Of course Frenchwomen have women friends—but they are a bit suspicious of having a foreign woman for a friend. You Americans have a spontaneity that inspires a lack of confidence in Frenchwomen."

So that's it! This wariness of other women, and the indisputable fact that American women are "spontaneous" (prompting suspicion) may be the reason for a certain secretiveness. After all, another woman is potential competition. If you compliment a Frenchwoman on her hairdo or manicure or necklace, she'll say thank you and smile, but you can bet your bottom dollar she won't open up and tell you who did the hair and nails or where she got the necklace. Why not? If she did, then you would know and you'd end up looking as good as she does. *Logique, non?*

Frenchwomen seem to avoid direct arguments with men. To wit, a conversation on rape I had at a dinner party with friends. This conversation would *never* take place in the United States, by the way. Jacques (not his real name—the guy definitely needs protection) maintained that it is impossible to rape a woman without her consent (!) and that marital rape is inconceivable. I tried to explain to him that if the woman refuses and the man goes ahead, it is rape. Our conversation went on and on, but we never came to an agreement, and he is now convinced that I am a crazy American feminist. Crazy, yes; feminist, moderately so (by American standards, not all that much; by French standards, quite a bit—it all depends on your point of view). The Frenchwomen present that evening somehow managed not to get involved in the debate.

I've been to zillions of dinner parties in France in different social classes and situations. I can assure you, dear women readers, that you see and hear things you would never even contemplate seeing or hearing in the United States. The Frenchwoman does not seem to feel the need to assert herself the way we American women do. She's too polite to act offended if she's left out. For example, at the home of a French intellectual, the host dominated the conversation and the women present, who were the wives of intellectuals but not intellectuals themselves, simply did not talk for the duration of the meal. All this is considered normal. What I am saying is, whatever the situation, whatever the social class, compared to American women, Frenchwomen accept the backseat. Period.

Whether the backseat is "good" or "bad," and whether they take it because it's the best option, is another story. Search me, as they say. If I knew the answer, I would have figured out the Frenchwoman. And as you can see, I haven't . . . yet.

In some ways, Frenchwomen are much less on their guard around men than we Americans are. They do delicious things, such as laugh at off-color jokes, and don't yell sexual harassment when complimented on their hairdo. They can disagree with a man—and keep their cool. So refreshing.

For example, in the rape conversation, the two Frenchwomen present let us (me and another non-Frenchwoman, who took Jacques's side) slug it out. They didn't sit there like dead fish, nor did they ostensibly change the conversation. I don't actually know what they were doing, so unobtrusive were they. But by not getting into the argument, they ensured that the dinner party remained a party and not a knock-down-drag-out. When I called to thank my hostess, I told her I hoped her husband wasn't too upset about our altercation. "Jacques?" She laughed. "He's crazy."

Clearly, conversations in France are very different from conversations in the United States. Maybe it's the wine, but somehow people can get into pretty heavy matters, even be diametrically opposed, but stop short of punching one another out. The good French hostess, of course, is there to smooth everything over. She's experienced at this. After all, she has to contend with her French husband, and any American wife married to a Frenchman can tell you that's no small matter.

I admire Frenchwomen: They have a real big secret they're not telling anyone. Their husbands must be babied. I adore Frenchmen (I married one, didn't I?), but

I wouldn't be alone in stating that their behavior is often totally weird and that their relationships with women are frequently, shall we say, not based on equality. This is why many women who are married to Frenchmen squirrel away money to buy things for their houses. Not because the guy doesn't have any money, but because he's going to have to make a comment. Nothing gets past him. So as not to have to hear it, the woman becomes a master at subterfuge. I know the case of an American woman who bought a piece of furniture without informing her French spouse, who had a tendency to give her a hard time about prospective purchases. It was a rather large dresser with three drawers. He never did notice—and it was at that point that the woman figured out that she was free to do what she wanted *without* egalitarian consulting. Seize the power!

There's a point to be made here about the Franco-American marriage. The American woman who has married a Frenchman finds herself in a rather odd position. She, who likes to think of herself as independent, freewheeling, and in power, finds herself at a triple disadvantage. She is on *his* territory, speaking *his* language, contending with *his* friends and family. Even if her dear husband happened to be the most democratic person in the world, she starts out with a few counts against her and spends an inordinate amount of her time simply defending herself. A few women never make it, divorce, and leave. Others become philosophical or assimilate, or both. Whatever the solution, it's a struggle.

This extends to small matters. Frenchmen want you to pack their bags, pick out their shirts, et cetera. When I complained about that, a female French friend of mine told me I shouldn't. If you pick out his clothes and pack his bag, she told me, you'll have a fighting chance of him looking nice, the way you want him to. I meditated on this and decided that she definitely had a point. I now, more or less, pack my husband's bag, and it's true, he does look better.

Another thing that fascinates me about Frenchwomen is their rather special mother-daughter relationship.

- My neighbor, who has two daughters, stopped on the street to talk to me the other day. She told me that her daughter was going to a private school in our area (only twenty minutes by car but a good hour on public transportation), so my neighbor gets up every morning at 7:00 A.M. to accompany her to school. The daughter is twenty.

- My sister-in-law and my mother-in-law phone each other every day and spend almost every weekend together in the country. I adore my mother, but, even if we weren't five thousand miles apart, I wonder what on earth we could find to say to each other every day.

- A French friend tells me about a woman friend of hers who would never think of buying a pair of shoes without asking her mother's approval. And the friend is fifty years old!

One explanation of the closeness of mothers and daughters is that almost half of the feminine population in France works, and many Frenchwomen have to turn to their mothers for child care (in spite of the excellent system of child-care centers that exists).

Another explanation is that, unlike in the States, many French young people do not travel far to university and either continue to live at home or stay in close physical proximity to their parents. This can also weigh on the daughter. A recent article in a French women's magazine pointed out how truly horrible adolescent daughters can be with their mothers, either by freezing them out or by running away from home—anything to get away from mom. A third explanation, which crosses my mind when I am up against a cold, superior-looking type of Frenchwoman, is that perhaps only their mothers can stand them—shame on me!

Mothers and daughters may have close links, but it doesn't seem to be a very sexy thing to have babies and then spend your life as a professional mother. The good side of this is that, in general, when you go to a French person's house for dinner, you will be spared the child routine, the horrors, say, of wading through an entire meal with a two-year-old you have to praise every two minutes, because children are really supposed to be seen (and then only at the appropriate time) and not heard.

French mothers seem to be bogged down by the duty side of motherhood (they would probably say that American mothers seem to hone in on the enjoyment part and disregard the discipline side). They bring the kids up, dress them well (my kids looked like ragamuffins compared with French kids, because they were dressed for fun, and fun for toddlers means dirt), feed them well, make sure they work well at school. The motherhood job seems to be a serious one indeed. An example: When I dropped my kids off at primary school, my parting words for the day always were, "Have fun!" Next to me, I would hear the French mothers admonishing their children to "be good" *(sois sage)*. *Voilà la dif-férence.*

Then there is the French mother-in-law. Since I have one (and we get along famously), I can say that there is only one real problem, and that is that she is French and I am American; so I am always wondering whether she is doing what she is doing because she is French, because she is my mother-in-law, or just because she'd do it anyway. (She's probably asking herself the same about me.)

Example: the lesson on how to wash leeks. My mother-in-law tells me they are to be split lengthwise, as opposed to being snipped up brutally, the way I do it. Salads: Wash them at least six times so there is no dirt left. Tomatoes: Don't just dump them into boiling water, as I do, and leave them to their fate; position them gently on a fork and swirl them around. And last but not least: dates. Never bite into a date without opening it up first. There might be a horrible insect or a worm in there. My love of dates has been spoiled forever.

Would an American mother-in-law have inculcated all these food tips in me? Of course, food is sacred to the French, and an American wife is always vaguely suspected of either poisoning her husband or allowing him to starve. Early on in my marriage, I invited my in-laws to visit us in our town, which is far from Paris. When my mother-in-law arrived with a baked chicken, I knew we still had a culture gap to close! (In her defense, I know now that she was just trying to save me trouble, but at the time, I think I had the persecution complex that many Americans married to Frenchmen have, and I entertained the darkest notions.)

The phone. I have been trying for years to communicate the fact that even if I lived in the same town with my mother in the States, I probably wouldn't call her every single day, not because I don't want to talk to her, but because I don't feel a duty to do that any more than she feels a duty to call me. My mother-in-law assents, but I know that in her heart of hearts she finds it hard to believe.

The American woman who has decided to marry a Frenchman and have his children is always conscious of the fact (whether she is made to feel conscious or she just feels conscious is another story) that, first of all, she took a man who could have married someone of his own nationality, and, second, she is not who she is but who the French think she is. Even her children think she is strange. I have suspected this for a long time in my own family as I watch the amused, tolerant, and sometimes embarrassed looks my boys cast at me when I am being so "un-French" in front of their French friends.

French sociologist Gabrielle Varro confirmed this for me when she wrote in her very interesting study *La femme transplantée: Une étude du mariage franco-américain en France et le bilinguisme des enfants (The Transplanted Woman: A Study of the Franco-American Marriage in France and the Bilingualism of Children)* that "in fact, the forty-year-old American woman is often much more 'extroverted,' more enthusiastic and demonstrative than her thirteen or fifteen year old child, who is exposed to an entirely different style of behavior and who has moreover a tendency to judge his American mother's behavior as extravagant and puerile." Varro is talking about the American woman who grew up in the United States in the fifties—but from my own experience, I could say that holds true of others, as well.

My kids were so afraid I would embarrass them that they would loudly announce the arrival of a friend the first half second they were in the door. "JEAN-PIERRE IS WITH ME," my oldest would yell, hoping I wouldn't be singing at the top of my voice or guffawing over the phone. He would then whisk the visitor back to his room and, later, whisk him out the door just as quickly.

In addition to mastering the Frenchwoman, I had to master the stereotype that some Frenchwomen have of American women. One popular French stereotype of the American woman is a lady with rollers in her hair and a rolling pin in her hand to bang on her husband's head should he dare get out of line. Her husband, of course, has been castrated a long time ago by this she-devil. This stereotype was reinforced by Lorena Bobbitt.

At a luncheon with a group of Parisian intellectuals, the conversation turned to American women. The Frenchwoman sitting at my left posed the inevitable question: "Is it true," she asked in feigned innocence, "that American women are loud and domineering?"

Had I been French, I would have immediately responded with something witty. But not having learned how to be what the French call *spirituel*—that is, how to let 'em have it without appearing heavy—I did not rise to the occasion.

If you live in France for any length of time, you need

to cultivate the art of being *vache*. *Vache* (yes, it means "cow"!) is a word that encompasses the concepts of petty, mean, spiteful. And just as, at their best, French-women can be witty, charming, and endlessly feminine, knowing how to converse, how to receive, how to dress, at their worst they can be *vache*. Even being *vache* is subtle. It is knowing how to utter that little phrase that can be interpreted however one wants. It is knowing how to send the dart without being transparently offensive.

Examples of *vache* comments include: "Oh, I like those living room curtains. I put the same ones in my little girl's bedroom." Or, a younger woman admiring an older woman's new diamond ring: "Ah, *l'alliance de la quarantaine*" (a ring your husband buys when you hit forty and he can finally afford it). Or how about "I've always loved you in that dress"?

Then there's the way Frenchwomen wear clothes. It's not that they have more clothes or better clothes. It's just that they manage to do something with them that ends up looking chic. My friend Anne-Marie has only about three outfits to her name, but she manages to make myriad different looks by cleverly using accessories. Of course this is a stereotype about Frenchwomen. Obviously, not all Frenchwomen know how to dress, but it is true that the ones who do know really understand what to do with little.

I love to watch Frenchwomen shop. They can be so terribly hostile. In a boutique one day, a more than middle-aged woman stooped to try on a pair of shoes. They didn't please her. The saleswoman brought another pair, and another. The lady looked her in the eye and boomed, "You aren't going to impose your taste on me. I'm the one who's imposing around here." I almost would have taken the poor saleslady's side if I hadn't remembered that, before the economic recession set in, you would go in to buy a pair of shoes and if you didn't walk out with a pair, even if they pinched your feet and looked terrible, you were treated like the poor cousin of someone's poor cousin.

I have observed that Frenchwomen do have a thing for shoes. On vacation with an American couple and a French couple, I watched the Frenchwoman tiptoe over ancient Turkish ruins in dainty open-toed heels, while the American woman and I clodded around in our dirty tennis shoes. Guess who looked better? By the same token, I have yet to see a French woman executive trodding along the streets of Paris in a business suit and tennis shoes. I decided to try out the nice shoe look one day and dressed in slacks and heels. The reaction of my American friends: "You've gone native!"

I love clothes and shoes, and I love the way the Frenchwomen select and wear them. But I must admit I quake upon entering boutiques. I steel myself for the saleswoman's inevitable lines: "This is the last belt [or skirt, or top] I have; you'd better take it." Or "I have the same belt [or skirt, or top]." I refrain from answering that if she has the same, I certainly don't want it. I note, as the years pass, that either I am getting bigger or the dresses and skirts are getting smaller. The French equivalent of size eight would seem to be the ideal dress size in France. A twelve is just all right, and a fourteen is bringing us to Elephant Land. What do you expect in a country where women pay so much attention to their *ligne* and their *toilette*?

Presumably, unlike me, Frenchwomen don't break out in a cold sweat when contemplating the joyous experience of shopping for clothes. They might, however, break out in a cold sweat, hives, or something else when they contemplate their horrendous underrepresentation in the National Assembly. Only 6 percent of the National Assembly is composed of women. In "macho" Spain, it's over twice that. Still, while a lot of Frenchwomen would like to be better represented, they aren't taking to the streets, and they don't hate the men who are there in their place.

Actually, maybe they should take to the streets. But then, horror of horrors, they might start resembling American feminists! That, one can fairly presume, is not something to which any Frenchwoman would aspire.

Interview with Philippe

HARRIET: *What difference do you think there would be if, instead of being married to an American woman, you were married to a Frenchwoman?*

PHILIPPE: *We wouldn't have a parliamentary debate on women's equality every morning before breakfast. She would just take control without saying a word.*

HARRIET: *What about issues such as who packs the bags?*

PHILIPPE: *She would do it, and make me pay for it without my ever knowing it.*

HARRIET: *What's another difference?*

PHILIPPE: *Frenchwomen will leave you alone when they see you are tired. For example, a Frenchwoman wouldn't persist in an interview like this when she sees how wiped out I am after a week of work. You, on the other hand, would interview me on my deathbed.*

HARRIET: *And yet another difference?*

PHILIPPE: *Only American women marry four times, kill off four husbands, and then go off to Europe and have fun.*

HARRIET: *Okay. Okay. Why is it that if a man is loud in France, no one pays any particular attention, but if a woman speaks or laughs loudly, everyone turns around and stares at her?*

PHILIPPE: *Because women are supposed to be more refined than men. Equality of sex in the States means that women should be as stupid as men.*

HARRIET: *Sexist . . .*

The French and Sex, Love, and Marriage

The way the French shop and prepare their food—as well as the obvious gusto with which they relish it—is an important cultural difference, one of the first and most lasting ones I encountered. But if food was a difference, just think of what I had to learn about the attitude of the French toward sex! Now that was a real eye-opener.

Sex is one area in which the cultural gap is *enormous*.

Probably the most obvious difference between the Americans and the French is the lack of prudishness with which the French talk about sex. After twenty years in France, I'm finally starting to get the jokes and even join in the laughter. Hey! I don't even blush when I walk by huge billboards with ladies in sexy bras or

men in sexy underpants or other various states of un-
dress. Progress!

But I was shocked when I first arrived. I thought an
off-color joke was a come-on. It took me twenty years
of slowly steeping in the ribald Rabelaisian tradition
to shuck my embarrassment and find a lot of this stuff
funny. Yes, I was prim indeed.

As a child growing up in the great American Midwest, I learned right off the bat that there were three
subjects one did not broach at the dinner table: sex, re-
ligion, and politics. Perhaps years of skirting the taboo
trio gave me a much better sense of humor about much
of what I hear at French dinner tables, where conversations are often *based* on one or more of the three forbidden fruits.

An example: There was a lively conversation in
which, amid much laughter, we admired two newborn
baby boys—their little hands and pretty skin and eyes,
right down to their penises, where a very factual allusion
was made in passing to the respective sizes. Up until that
point, I had been translating much of the lighthearted
banter for my brother-in-law, who was visiting from
Chicago. But somehow, my midwestern upbringing got
in the way of a truthful rendering of the penis comparison. I knew that he, a fellow midwesterner, would have
been as embarrassed as I was. Something would definitely have been lost in translation.

Since they are not puritanical, the French talk about

sex very openly. This does not mean that they are a nation of sex fiends; it just means that there is no stigma attached to the discussion of sex in mixed company (or in general). Of course, that depends on who's discussing it and how. A reality check here: Most French people don't sit around talking about sex. They also talk about philosophy, politics, money (not all that much), food, and wine (a lot).

In France, sexual innuendos abound in conversations. These sexual references, many of which are puns or word associations, are much more frequent than dirty jokes. Locker room conversations, I am told, are looked down on. I mean, who needs to "talk dirty" when it's all out in the open? (On this score, if I may add an editorial comment, I think the French are saner than the Anglo-Saxons.)

"We're not puritanical and hence we're less hypo-critical about sex than the Americans are," remarked one Frenchwoman with a certain pride.

You can say that again.

To see how really unpuritanical the French are, you just have to look at their ads. Of course everyone sells consumer goods by using sex, but the French excel at it. French publicist Jacques Séguéla calls American publicity "efficient and aggressive" . . . to the saturation point. In contrast, he says that French advertising is "instinctive, passionate, sentimental, romantic, in brief, warm."

Sometimes the ads are just "warm," as he says. Sometimes they're hot.

One of the best-known and -remembered ones was a TV ad for Perrier. In it, the famous little green bottle is stroked by the expert red-nailed fingers of a woman who does not appear on-screen. The bottle, which starts out at 8 ounces, grows to 12 ounces under the expert palpatation. Then it grows and grows even more, until at one liter, it literally explodes its liquid into the air. "This spot," concluded one French magazine, "was like the butter scene in *Last Tango in Paris.*"

Well, we certainly didn't see anything like *that* when I was growing up in Iowa. And we certainly didn't see what I saw one day while thumbing through the photo album of a very close French friend, one of the most conventionally bourgeois people you would ever hope to run across. There sat my girlfriend, barebreasted, on a beach, with her two little girls at her side. I wasn't surprised that she had been bare-breasted on the beach. What surprised me was that she had included the photo in the family album, which everyone would look at, including her own mother! My immediate reaction to the photos was proof to me that my midwestern primness has not entirely deserted me.

By the same token, I used to be shocked by a lot of the conversations going on around me. But I now see that rather than turning my children into sex maniacs, the frankness with which sex is discussed has made them remarkably relaxed about it. They talk about sex like they talk about breakfast cereal. Of course I am speaking about a milieu of freethinkers; in a traditional family, this freedom of speech is hardly the rule. Some French families are as prudish as any basic midwestern family, or more, believe it or not.

When translated, many French words and expressions sound absolutely terrible, much worse than they are in French. For example, an overnight bag is sometimes referred to as a "*baise-en-ville*" (screwing in town, literally). French author Jean-Claude Carrière cataloged hundreds of synonyms for the various parts of the body in his book *Les mots et la chose: Le grand livre des petits mots inconvenants (The Words and the Thing: the Big Book of Little Indecent Words)*. Among the synonyms for the male organ: *le phallus, le pénis, la verge*, but also ancient words such as *le vit* (donkey's penis), *le dard* (stinger), *l'épinette* (little thorn), *le braquemart* (short sword), and *l'arbalète* (crossbow). Add to this *la bite, la pine, la queue, le paf, le truc, le légume d'amour* (vegetable of love!) and you'll begin to get just a small idea of this vast subject. The chapter on synonyms for the male organ is eighteen pages long!

The open way in which people talk about sex is one thing that struck me as an enormous cultural difference. Another difference I discovered was in the relationship between men and women.

First, the facts: Frenchwomen didn't get the right to vote until 1945, ninety-six years after men had it. They are still paid less than men and are underrepresented in all walks of life, in spite of a few notable exceptions. And, let's face it, a lot of Frenchmen (especially politicians) are male chauvinist pigs. One has only to view the almost all-male composition of the French National Assembly to see that women have definitely not "made it" yet in French society.

But one can't leave it at that.

What continues to strike me is that Frenchmen and Frenchwomen like one another's company. They don't seem to feel any need for systematic antagonism.

There's a lightness in male-female relationships that we Anglo-Saxons don't always get, at least not at first. Visiting Paris for the first time, the beautiful young American daughter of a dear friend of mine told me she was upset at being followed down the street by a French fellow. "But," she said, a bit mystified, "when he saw I wasn't interested, he just said, 'Good-bye,' smiled, and went on his way."

That's because the rules of the game are different. "Frenchmen seek seduction, not domination," a French gentleman friend told me. This world traveler and woman-watcher observed that in the States, letting a woman pass in front of you, opening a car door, paying the bill at a restaurant, giving the *baisemain* (kissing her hand—horrors!), which only a decadent European would do anyway, are all viewed with the utmost suspicion. "The idea that a man would take a woman to dinner, do all of the above, and not try to bed her is inconceivable in the States," he told me with a Gallic shrug of disdain.

One reason that Frenchwomen do not fear male-female games—or the opposite sex—is that flirtation does not imply or require follow-up. Flirting, he explained, is the same as strolling. "It's for the pleasure of it. What might come afterward is fun if it happens, but it is not the primary goal."

Some people maintain that the relationship between Frenchmen and Frenchwomen is very special. As far as I can see, there is a tacit agreement between the two sexes. As long as women regiment the action from behind the scenes, which they do, everybody gets along. Frenchwomen understand this and they're much too clever to get into a confrontation with men. The "special" relationship between men and women in France is based on the premise that if you don't rock my boat, I won't rock yours (my opinion).

In her book *XY: De l'identité masculine (XY: Of Masculine Identity)* French author and sociologist Elisabeth Badinter maintains that the uniqueness of male-female relationships in France comes in part from the fact that Frenchmen acknowledge their feminine side. A case in point: Frenchmen don't see buying lingerie for their girlfriends as a threat to their manliness, *au contraire*. Badinter says the Scandinavian man is "soft" and the American man is "tough," whereas the Frenchman is the perfect combination.

"The American type of tough guy has no equivalent in France," she writes. "Of course, we have the patriarch, the ordinary macho, but not the extraordinary supermacho." Rambo and the Terminator, she says, are definitely American specialties.

Ah, so that "feminine side" explains why I have a soft spot for Frenchmen, thought I, after reading Badinter's theory. They do have an endearing side. I exclude, of course, all those macho dudes behind the wheels of their teeny-weeny R5s or Peugeot 305s or the guys who yell "*Connasse*" (translation unprintable) out their car window: They don't look to me like they're "acknowledging their feminine side" one bit.

"What," asked an American man one day, upon learning that a mutual friend was going to marry a Frenchman, "do these Frogs have that we don't?" To be sure, not every Frenchman is Gérard Depardieu or Jean Reno—but still, there are a few things that Frenchmen have in common that make them so . . . French.

For one thing, a sense of seduction. As a journalist friend of mine remarked, a Frenchman is capable of flirting with you over the phone, sight unseen. She recounts a phone interview with the late Yves Montand in which he was positively seducing her with his charm. What did he care if she was sixty-five or twenty-two? He had never seen her and probably never would—but why not be agreeable just in case? The point is that, as any self-respecting French male would, he wanted to win her

over. The sexual tension, the recognition that one person is a man and that the other is a woman, permeates
life in France. There is none of this "Oh, we're doing
business; we're all neuter" stuff. No one, thank God,
forgets what sex he or she is.

France has not succumbed to the politically correct
movement in the area of sex (thank goodness). Thus, a woman is
delighted, not shocked, when a man notices her new dress,
and the man is not afraid that an innocent compliment will lead
to a complaint of sexual harassment. Hey! But then no
self-respecting Frenchwoman would consider herself "victimized"
by a man's paying attention to her. *Au contraire!*

Many Frenchmen have a wonderful sense of humor
about the whole game of flirting. France is probably the
one country an attractive single woman can live in
peacefully, because a woman is allowed to take or leave
the attentions men lavish on her. To be more explicit: If
you tell a man to bug off, he will. He was just trying,
and if he succeeds in getting your attention or making
you laugh, well, it was worth the attempt. One American woman who lived with a Frenchman for many
years told me, "As far as making you feel like a woman,
the Frenchman wins hands down." And she added, "The
French are the only men I've ever known who can make

love with their shoes and socks on in the heat of the moment, because they're not concerned about whether they look ridiculous or not." For this woman, the American male, on the other hand, might get a better score both on treating women as equals and the use of soap, two points on which not all Frenchmen would get a passing grade.

In a general sense, soap or no soap, Frenchmen are not afraid of body contact. It's not unusual to see grown men giving each other kisses and bear hugs. They're not afraid to go into a lingerie shop and choose underwear for their partner. (You can see them in the shops, earnestly studying the different colors and shapes.) An Englishman who wanted to get a pretty slip or bra for his wife said he finally couldn't bring himself to do it because his sister, who ran a lingerie shop in England, had confided to him that the men who came in the boutique to look at the underwear were trying it on for themselves! He ended up buying his wife a painting.

What about the myth of the French lover? One American woman who lived with a Frenchman for twelve years puts it bluntly: "The French don't wash enough to be sexy. For me," she explains, "cleanliness is next to sexiness. Americans like to take a shower before they get started and the French just like to dive into it without having had a shower in three days." This, of course, is a generalization, and I've heard stories of very clean (by American standards) Frenchmen. But it is perhaps true to say that for a Frenchman, squeaky-clean leaves nothing much to desire. Not for himself, nor for his mistress. Wasn't it Napoléon who on his way back from battle wrote to Josephine, "Don't wash; I'm on my way"?

"I think Frenchmen are much more charming and gentlemanly," a young American who is engaged to a Frenchman told me. "On the other hand, since they are more gentlemanly, they want you to be more womanly. And that's hard. You can be a knockout California girl in a T-shirt and jeans, but in general that won't be enough. They notice everything. In a way, it's nice, and in another way, it's scrutinizing and an extra pressure on the woman." And she added, "Another big difference here is that everything is out in the open. Sex magazines are right out on the shelves and the men leaf through them and buy them without sneaking around about it. In the States, if a guy is looking at one of those magazines, it means he's got some hang-up. His interest is not natural or shared. It is much more suppressed."

As far as intimacy is concerned, another American woman married to a Frenchman told me that in her opinion Frenchmen are "better at intimacy and not embarrassed about sex; it's not a hang-up for them. When they experiment with sex, it's because they want to try something new, but not at all in a prurient way."

On the other hand, one American woman told me, "Frenchmen have enormous egos. For example, if they want to take you to bed and you don't want to go right away and are thinking it over, they make you feel like you are abnormal, or unnatural. That way, the burden is all on you and they retain their ego."

Another opinion about Frenchmen comes from an American therapist who works with French-American couples. "Frenchmen tend to build walls around themselves," she says. "They try not to let people know what they are really like. It is difficult for them to question themselves, because of their upbringing, so they are constantly on the defensive. I feel that it is very threatening for them not to be like other people, even though they can be iconoclastic in intellectual arguments. But as for the rest, their humor evaporates the moment you swing from the norm. They are very self-protective." She says that when she works with Frenchmen in a therapy situation, she is careful to show them that she respects this "self-defense." Her words clearly come from close observation. Can anyone imagine a group of Frenchmen in one of those male-bonding groups that have cropped up in the States? No way. Touchy-feely hasn't hit the French male yet.

In spite of their sometimes monstrous egos and their "self-protection," Frenchmen often entice foreign women (just look at how many American women in Paris are married to Frenchmen). A divorced Australian woman who works in a large multinational company and dates both Frenchmen and Americans told me that she finds it a relief to be able to joke around rather explicitly with her French male colleague because "he just laughs and doesn't think of our conversation as a come-on, which the Americans do." She, like other observers, says she likes the "dose of femininity" in French males.

Badinter says that Frenchmen don't need this tough-guy aspect because they have better relationships with their mothers. Her explanation is that the French mother hasn't smothered her son the way the American or German mother has, nor has she abandoned him the way the English mother does by sending him away to boarding school. "Less prisoners of their mothers, our sons hate women less," she writes. Interesting theory.

Even the feminist movement in France, says Badinter, was not characterized by the rupture with men that has been seen in the States. "I am not saying that France has escaped a patriarchy or the oppression of women, but I observe a difference in the nature of it . . . there is less hate between the sexes here than elsewhere."

I agree on the last point, but I *love* the part about the French mothers. A lot of American women married to Frenchmen might contest the point about Frenchmen being "less prisoners" of their moms. Actually, some Frenchmen would like their wives to *be* their moms, or at least do things as well as she did.

My French husband would like me to PACK HIS BAG when we go on trips. Since he doesn't pack my bag, I don't see why I should pack his. This is American equality, right? The last time this happened, we were on our way to the Norman coastal town of Etretat for a late-fall weekend. "You did bring my toothbrush and razor, didn't you?" he asked, glancing over my way casually. Actually, for once in my life, I *had* ventured to pack his bag, congratulating myself all the while on my open-mindedness, my *largesse d'esprit*. But of course I had forgotten the razor, toothbrush, and just about everything else that was essential.

After twenty years in France, I can't get excited anymore about the issue of bag packing. I figure that (a) he doesn't have all that much time, (b) he is absolutely not interested in what he wears, and (c) he's bound to look better if I do it. Maybe I have become French after all. I'm in good company at least. Bernadette Chirac, wife of the French president, recently told reporters that she *always* packs Jacques's valise. He wouldn't think of going on any trip, official or otherwise, without her preparing his suitcase.

Could you be thinking at this point that Frenchmen are also looking for a mother when they wed? Well . . .

It's interesting to consider what the Frenchman looks for in a woman. Basically, he wants a sexy supermom. In one poll, Frenchmen said they preferred women in silk underwear to women in cotton underwear (no surprise there); a shy demeanor, as opposed to a bold one; a chic suit rather than shorts; and an accomplished housewife rather than a social butterfly or perfect hostess. Sixty-nine percent said they preferred an intelligent woman; 72 percent said a housewife; and 68 percent chose a good cook. In other words, they want it all: a perfectly groomed, intelligent, unassuming creature who manages to run a perfect home and cook terrific food.

Now, about the "shy demeanor" bit. In the United States, women are encouraged to speak up. Not so in France. Even if the men aren't talking just to one another, it is clear that the women are consciously or unconsciously taking second place, harmonizing with the men but not daring to go out on a limb or take the lead. I mention this because as a forthright lively American female, I have to make a mammoth effort to zip up my mouth at formal French dinner parties so as not to come on as being too aggressive. A *definite* cultural gap.

A terrible thing did happen one night, though. At a dinner party given by a Frenchman and his American wife, I found myself with several very entertaining American women who were there with their French husbands. Even before, and certainly after, several drinks, we American women got together and started loudly laughing and having a good time. The Frenchmen were excluded. We were having such a fun, boisterous time that we had *forgotten* them. And they, totally unused to such behavior, didn't really know what to do. It was very impolite.

There are a lot of generalizations you can make about the French and most of them probably would not stand up half the time, but I can safely say that never would you see that kind of conduct from a group of Frenchwomen, especially Parisian women. First of all, they don't enjoy one another's company that much. That sounds nasty, but what I mean is that since the French are not only not taught to smile but think that the generalized smile is something reserved for dolts, you can't really tell whether they are having the time of their lives or are bored out of their minds. Second, French women bond in a quieter, more personal way. Third, they never drink too much and hence don't let go. To their everlasting credit, one might be tempted to say.

So we American women present that night were very ashamed and vowed to toe the line at future social occasions.

Male-female relationships in France seem to be decidedly different from the way they are in the States. If, by some quirk of fate, you find yourself in a Franco-American marriage, you get the fun of observing all of these considerable cultural gaps firsthand—and don't let anyone tell you there aren't any (or many).

All of these cultural gaps are exacerbated in an intercultural marriage. Marriage is hard enough as it is, and intercultural marriages can be even harder because of incomprehension due to cultural differences. "I think that all the differences in traditional marriages are even harder in intercultural marriages," family counselor Jill Bourdais, an American who has lived in Paris with her French husband for over twenty years, told me. She offered in-laws as an example of cultural differences. When Americans marry, she says, there is the shared assumption that the in-laws might be difficult, and that you don't necessarily have to see them. "The expectation here is that you have to go to your mother-in-law's house once a week rain or shine, and this comes as a shock to the American partner. And once you get there, you often find that you are the child and that the mother-in-law runs the show for everyone."

One American who goes to the south of France regularly to visit her in-laws complained that the mother-in-law wouldn't let anyone, not her or her children, out of the house when it was too hot. "So there we are, prisoners inside the house, because she has proclaimed that that's the way it's going to be." I must admit that the first time I heard my late father-in-law calling for the children *(les enfants)*, I thought he was addressing my two young sons. *Mais non!* He was addressing me and my husband. *We* were the children.

Child raising can be another major area of conflict for Franco-American couples. Confides one friend who is still happily married: "I think our biggest conflict was over bringing up children. The French have this Catholic attitude of original sin in which they see the child as being born bad and needing to be straightened up. My husband—but this is his character and perhaps not because he is French—is quick to criticize and slow to praise." She laughs: "It's not that he's mean, but he was brought up that way himself." And she continues: "I was afraid the kids would grow up hating their father. A lot of French fathers don't horse around with their kids, take them camping, or be a pal. They retain more of a distant relationship."

I, too, was surprised by the distance my husband adopted toward our children when they were very young. Having been brought up in a household where the children didn't even dare open their mouths at the dinner table, his only wish was that his own children would do the same. Boy, was he disappointed. The happy postscript to this is that in spite of not being the television image of the father out camping with his sons or playing touch football, my French husband has been a remarkable father to his children. (I am the supersoft touch, whereas he, fortunately, won't, as we say in the Midwest, take any guff from them.) The funniest part of it is that somehow subliminally the "Don't open your mouth at the table" message did eventually get through—and now we have a hard time getting them to talk when there's company. Figure that one out. It must be their French genes surfacing.

Another American woman attributes most of the problems in her marriage to the difference in the way she and her husband see their only child. The French father is stern, often reprimanding his son for not working hard enough at school. The American mother's main concern is that the child is having fun and enjoying himself.

Another difference some American women married to Frenchmen point out is that, in their French families, it is up to the children to call their grandparents. In France, it seems that it is up to the younger people to initiate contacts with the elders, including children to parents, rather than vice versa.

"I realized that cultural differences were vital in our misunderstanding," Julie told me over a cup of coffee in a café. In the late-morning quiet of the café in the sixteenth arrondissement, while waiters made ready for the noon crush of eaters, this attractive American divorcée in her mid-forties told me about her own experience in France. Married to a Frenchman for twenty years, separated for eight years, and just recently divorced, she said that she spent an inordinate amount of time and energy maintaining her Americanness, in spite of having mastered the language. "This translated into an enormous amount of aggressivity. I was fighting for my Americanness even though my ex-husband spoke perfect English, went to New York more than I did, and saw my friends. I tried very hard to be French, learned the rules, spoke the language, got along well with my in-laws." She came to realize that cultural differences figured prominently in their misunderstandings.

Now with an American boyfriend, she says that the aggressivity has disappeared. "I had to fight twenty years for my identity, and now that I am with an American boyfriend, I find that I can really enjoy France," says Julie, who has now lived longer in France than in the United States. Reflecting on her past, she says that "when you come and you are very young, you are absolutely dependent on the man you married and you don't become a woman." Another problem, perhaps independent of the cultural factor, was that she and her husband didn't realize the importance of getting away together as a couple, that the couple comes first. "All this fed into my wanting to fight for my American bit, and the more I felt out of it, the more I was." For her, "the middle road, which not many people get to, is simply saying, 'I'm me and you're you.'"

It's often hard, though, when attitudes are so different. One of these bones of contention is what family therapist Jill Bourdais calls the general attitude toward the outside world. "In the United States, you assume people are nice until proven wrong. Here, you're almost a criminal until proven trustworthy. In the States, a couple wants to enjoy new people, but here you don't just casually invite someone because they are nice. You need to find out more about them, their social status, and there is a complete lack of spontaneity."

Other sensitive areas in intercultural marriages include lack of communication due to language differences or social codes. Outgoing Americans are generally disturbed when they go to dinner parties and realize they have to button up their mouths on almost every single subject that could reveal something personal about themselves. Otherwise, the person next to them could think he's been mistaken for their therapist.

Then there's the guilt complex about money. (I'll go into more detail on this subject in the next chapter.) Many of my American friends married to Frenchmen say the same thing: Their spouse makes them feel culpable about spending the household *sous*. "We're going to eat noodles this month," wails Pierre to his wife, who is honestly terrified when this successful lawyer tells her he thinks that they may not make it through the month. She will spend the next day thinking of selling her jewels or getting a job. That night, however, he comes home and hits her with "I just saw the most fantastic pair of diamond earrings I'd like to buy you."

My friend and I commiserate with each other about this yo-yo behavior. I tell her that my French husband, one of the most generous people I know, has done this to me for years. The tense look, the tight voice, the desperate air—how many times did I think we would be going to debtors' prison because I had splurged on a new tablecloth? And then he would gallantly invite me out to dinner. Another American friend tells me that the guilt complex is routine practice in her home, too. Her husband went so far as to make sure she didn't have a checking account (she spends money like water, I must admit), and so the only money she could get would be by going through him, the Great Provider.

Does this sound like the Dark Ages? It is.

However, after two decades of observing and studying the phenomenon, I have finally figured it out. These men are Latin: They are just exteriorizing their worry, blowing off steam, so to speak. *Frenchwomen know this.* We literal-minded American wives sit there biting our fingernails, cursing ourselves for being so irresponsible, and becoming convinced we'll end up either poor or in prison, or both. What we don't understand is that the poor guy just had a hard day at the office and simply wants to express himself. Being the nearest and dearest, we're in the direct line of fire. Since relationships are not equal, we have to listen to the histrionics—and they are histrionics—as part of the deal.

I repeat: If the American wife thinks she will be getting into a union based on honey-dewed consensus, she is wrong. The French love to bicker, and a quarrel is not seen as anything particularly threatening. In a French couple, separation is tolerated, too. In August, the woman often takes off for the seashore with the kids, leaving the husband behind (the famous "August husbands"). No one is horrified by the idea of not being together. A little relief is seen as a positive, not a negative, element. Still, one American man confessed in counseling that he resented his French wife's going off with the children and leaving him behind.

As time goes on, I feel myself becoming more and more French—or less and less American—in my relationship to my husband. I don't even listen when he rants and raves. Typical Latin overdramatization, I tell myself. It's when he's silent that I worry. As for dinner table conversations where there are sexual allusions, I shut my mouth, listen to the jokes, and join in the laughter—but I don't translate. Some things you just can't do.

Interview with Philippe

HARRIET: *What about the criticism by some American women that Frenchmen don't automatically take a shower before sex?*

PHILIPPE: *Sex and soap don't match. To excite an American woman, you have her smell a bar of soap. To excite a Latin woman, you offer the jungle smell.*

HARRIET: *What about that mysterious French invention, the bidet?*

PHILIPPE: *The French wonder why other countries don't have them. How can the people be clean?*

HARRIET: *What does a Frenchman look for in a woman?*

PHILIPPE: *A Frenchwoman or an American woman?*

HARRIET: *Ha-ha. Why are there so many dirty jokes and sexual innuendos in French conversations?*

PHILIPPE: *This isn't just French—it's Latin. But French culture, from the Gauls to Rabelais to San Antonio, is filled with sexual allusions. You Anglo-Saxons are the ones who have a hang-up, not us. Calvin, who incidentally was a Frog, got you people all messed up.*

HARRIET: *I thought he was Swiss.*

PHILIPPE: *No, like Jules Verne, he was French.*

HARRIET: *Chauvinist . . .*

The French and Money

Food, sex, and the Frenchwoman, all the surprises found therein pale in comparison to what I found to be the attitude of the French toward money. It could best be summed up as secretive. Here goes for an attempt at an explanation.

In a country where you can wax eloquent on almost anything, there's one subject that everyone avoids. A Frenchman will go on for hours about the best way to prepare a *canard à l'orange* or the attributes of haute couture, but when it comes to lucre, he clams up.

The basic attitude toward money seems to be this: the less said about it, the better. A French journalist told me that he once phoned the head of one of France's wealthiest families to interview him for an article he was writing.

The person refused, saying, "*Ce qui est bien ne fait pas du bruit; ce qui fait du bruit n'est pas bien.*" ("What is good doesn't make noise; what makes noise isn't good.")

This attitude toward money carries over into political life in France. The Anglo-Saxons are world specialists in the sex scandal. The more realistic French don't expect any politician to be perfect. They couldn't care less about Anita Hill and Clarence Thomas or Monica Lewinsky and Bill Clinton. The basic point of view in France is that a politician's private life (that is, his sex life) is his *private* life and none of anyone's (including the taxpayer/voter's) business. For years, French journalists knew that President François Mitterrand had a mistress and a daughter by her. He even admitted it in an interview, saying, "So what?" and the matter was dropped. The scandals under Mitterrand were *financial* scandals.

Nobody cares if a French politician has a mistress, or two or three, and he certainly wouldn't care if this was discovered. In fact, he'd be proud. But there is one thing he would certainly not like, and that would be for people to know how much money he is making or have his tax form published for the world to see. Why?

"Money is like sex," writes French journalist and TV personality François de Closets. "It is talked about in general and not in particular, in the abstract and not with personal examples." Of course the French love to joke about sex—but I've rarely if ever heard a joke about money. "The silence of the French when it comes to money," observes de Closets, "is not that of indifference, but of passion. It translates kind of a secret and guilty obsession . . . a censored desire, that is to say a taboo in the strongest sense of the word."

This doesn't mean that the French don't like money in all its forms, from the gold brick under the pillow to investments in real estate. But all this is laden with a terrible collective guilt complex. "The specificity of the French attitude [toward money]" writes François de Closets, "is not his love of it, but in his repression of this love."

Other than the nouveau riche, who don't know how to act, most Frenchmen have figured out that it's better to hide wealth than flaunt it. One of the reasons for this is to avoid the taxman; the other is to avoid sheer jealousy.

Jealousy comes in many forms:

- A journalist from a French magazine reported that he joined a young man for a ride around Paris in his brand-new flaming-red Porsche. Sure enough, they were stopped by the police for verification of their identity papers, which the French must always have on them just in case the police want to check them for some reason. The young man said he had been stopped several times and each time the police would say, "Anyway, with a car like that, you can pay the fine."

- I might never have believed that even the police are motivated by jealousy had I not seen the different way they acted toward my husband on two separate occasions. The first time, he was dressed in business clothes and driving our Renault 25, the "big," expensive car. The police stopped us during a routine checkup and, in spite of our total innocence, were much nastier than they needed to be, which was not at all.

  The second time we were stopped, the situation was entirely different—and a priori much worse. My husband had on a leather jacket and corduroy slacks and was driving my small, inexpensive, pigeon-dropping-splattered, sap-covered Citroën. In a fit of very Parisian impatience, he had pulled over a white line and hit a cop on a motorcycle. In one split second, I had a vision of our children as orphans as he and I were hauled off to prison for life. Instead, the cop got up from where he had fallen, brushed himself off, and just smiled. The only explanation for this totally bizarre behavior that we could find was that the cop would have had a hard time explaining what *he* was doing on the wrong side of the white line. But the fact that we were dressed casually in an unassuming little car certainly didn't hurt our case.

- In the neighborhood of nouveaux riches where I live, the merchants have marked their prices up to almost twice what they are elsewhere in this particularly expensive suburb. Even the baguette, that staff of life, costs more than anywhere else in town. If you are stupid enough not to ask the price of whatever it is you covet, you're sure to get a very big surprise indeed. The attitude is—and at least one boutique owner has admitted to it—If they can pay, we'll soak them.

- Friends of mine, a young Parisian lawyer and his American wife, decided to live for a year in a charming village in the southwest where his parents own a home. They bought a sizable old barn of a house, did repairs, and even added a swimming pool, to the horror of the locals. This was not the prodigal son returning home; it was an upstart Parisian flaunting his wealth. When the young lawyer, who, on top of everything else, is good-looking and blessed with eloquence and warmth, would visit the locals in his Mercedes, he would hear such comments as "Is it normal to have so much money?"

Successful French publicist Jacques Séguéla writes, "The Frenchman is the most illogical person in the world. He spends his life running after his success but the success of others bothers him. Worse, it makes him aggressive. In other countries, winning gains you the esteem of your compatriots. Here, it's the best way to lose it."

Or, in the words of the fictional character Major Thompson, created by French humorist Pierre Daninos: "The American pedestrian who sees a millionaire going by in a Cadillac secretly dreams of the day that he will get in his own. The French pedestrian who sees a millionaire in a Cadillac secretly dreams of the day that he will be able to get him out of the car so that he will walk like everyone else."

One reason for jealousy is that since no one talks about money openly, no one knows for sure what other people make and hence have totally false ideas. One day, my husband, a banker, was with two of his young employees. As they were early for an appointment, my husband suggested that they walk around the Place Vendôme, where they could admire the wonderful jewelry shops—Chaumet, Mauboussin, Van Cleef & Arpels. "Not only were they thoroughly uninterested," he reported, laughing, "but one of them turned to me and said, 'I see you are very rich to be so interested in jewels.'" Jealousy? Perhaps just boredom or a bad mood. But certainly a good deal of naïveté about his employer's standard of living!

Jealousy is only one of the reasons the French
don't like to talk about money. Following is another
very good one: fear of the big bad wolf—*le fisc*
(the tax inspector).

Besides jealousy, one reason not to flaunt wealth is fear of the taxman. In the city of Lyon, where there is a traditional wealthy bourgeoisie, affluent families drive the oldest, most run-down cars they can find, leave the Rolls-Royce hidden in a garage thirty miles from the city, wear dowdy clothes, and don't open their apartments to strangers. The other reason for this is that showing your wealth marks you forever as a nouveau riche, not a desired status for people who have "old money."

I underestimated the fear of the taxman until one night a friend came to dinner with a couple of shoe boxes filled to the brim with gold bullion, a gift from his dying uncle. I thought it was so funny that I told the story at a dinner party one night in the presence of the friend, who immediately turned several shades of green.

My husband took me aside later and told me that you must never, but never, talk about such personal matters. After all, how did we know that there wasn't a tax inspector at the table? "The taxman," says French journalist Isabelle Quenin, "is the big bad wolf. In fact, as soon as Frenchmen start talking about money, they have the feeling they are already in court."

Why such fear? For one thing, *many* people cheat on taxes, the attitude being that if you don't, you're not quite normal. Why? French journalist François de Closets explains the historical reasons for the French propensity to cheat the government and then fear the taxman. Under the laws of the ancien régime, king, queen, nobility, and clergy were exempted from taxes, which were taken from the masses of poor peasants! The idea that "someone on top" is out to get them has never left the national conscience.

This explains why secrecy and dissimulation became the means of dealing with the fear of having everything taken away (I still know French people who hide money inside the mattress). The French love for gold bullion also stems from the idea "They can't take this from me." When de Closets was researching his book back in the 1970s, it was estimated that the French people—not the French government—owned one-quarter of the world's gold reserves!

The taxman's visit, incidentally, may in actual fact be motivated by denunciation, from an unhappy client or a former husband or wife, an angry neighbor. If you tell on someone and the tax inspector finds an irregularity, you will get 10 percent of the fine in cash—not a bad deal. "The traffic cops and tax inspectors are universally detested in France," says Isabelle Quenin. "And the tax inspector is not only detested, but feared."

The French are highly taxed but live in a society where a sixteen-week maternity leave, a minimum of five weeks of annual vacation and often much more, and all kinds of other advantages are taken for granted. Yet, as de Closets writes, "The idea remains anchored that the fairest state is the one which takes the least, and all the demonstrations from other countries do nothing to change this."

The French yell and scream and cheat on their taxes, but how many would settle for roads with potholes, entire city neighborhoods that look like a bomb has hit them, and little or no insurance for health or old age? If you told the average Frenchman that he could pay fewer taxes and live in the United States but that he would have to put up with all of the above, you can bet he would prefer to live in France, screaming all the while.

Of course, some people scream less than others, as all Frenchmen do not pay taxes on the same scale. If you are a journalist, photographer, music and drama critic, airplane pilot or mechanic, you get an automatic 30 percent reduction off your taxes. Musicians, heads of orchestras, dramatic or lyric artists get 25 percent knocked off. Stockbrokers and seamstresses for the great couture houses, and very precise categories, such as people in the Loire who "work at home filing bicycle frames" get 20 percent whacked off. Still others get anywhere from 5 percent to 15 percent off, depending on where they live and what they do. For example, clock-makers get 5 percent off if they own their own tools; printers of newspapers who have to work at night are allowed a 5 percent deduction, as well.

Some of these reductions are restricted to a certain geographical location, such as the Loire bicycle filers: others are in effect all over France, wherever the profession is practiced. If you're just a normal salaried worker belonging to none of the above categories, you pay the whole lot. No wonder people are jealous!

Of course, not all Frenchmen think it is normal to cheat on taxes. Various polls show—not unsurprisingly—that those classes of people who find it more difficult or even impossible to cheat disapprove of cheaters. Those who have more ways to find loopholes (shopkeepers, people in independent professions) approve of cheating. As people grow older, they find it less normal to cheat.

Of course cheating goes on everywhere, but cheating in France is special because it is often so petty. I'll never forget the first time I got the wrong change on a baguette. I counted and recounted, thinking, What interest is there in cheating someone out of ten centimes?

For a long time, I really did think that the petty

cheating I was subject to was due to my accent. After all, an American accent is *the* accent not to have when you want to buy something. The price shoots up anywhere from 5 to 95 percent. But it wasn't because of my accent, I found out. In fact, most small shopkeepers are honest. But the ones who aren't select their victims on a random basis, not by their accents. In my neighborhood, which, as I said, is filled with people who are nouveau riche, the shopkeepers have decided that since many people don't seem to be counting, they may as well take advantage of the situation. This went on for years, until suddenly one day they found they had no more clients—people were deserting the neighborhood to buy in big supermarkets, where the prices are marked.

Knowing what the situation is, we hardly ever buy anything in this neighborhood. But one day, my son, in a fit of adolescent hunger, went downstairs to buy a box of cookies at the small chain grocery store in the street. He looked at his change and saw that they hadn't given him the correct amount: Five centimes, admittedly a minuscule sum, were missing. He didn't say anything and came back home, where he immediately regretted not having said anything, for it wasn't the first time that a "mistake" had been made. He returned to the store and politely told them about the error. The answer: "Why didn't you say anything then?" and "Anyway, you don't look as if you need five centimes." After that, the *coup final* from the irate grocer: "I've been in the grocery business twenty years and no little creep like you is go-ing to tell me how to run my business."

Culture Shock! I thought the customer was always right, if you want to keep his business, that is. *Mais non.* You complain about something and the merchant bawls *you* out.

The denouement of the above story is that I charged into the store the next day and closely followed my hus-band's instructions for bawling the storekeeper out. I was not, he told me, to engage in any discussion with him. After making sure that he knew that I knew what had gone on, I was to leave the store immediately with the line "*Je ne discute pas avec quelqu'un comme vous.*" ("I don't talk to people like you.") I executed according to instructions. Had I let myself go, I would have been exposed to a fishmonger's tirade, my husband told me. This way, I would emerge the offended winner. He was right. (And to my great satisfaction, a few years later, the entire chain went bankrupt!)

I had won that particular battle but not the war. I had to get used to counting my change in the stores on my street—and to the idea that the customer is not only not always right but almost always wrong.

Dear readers, in case you are wondering if I am down on the French, you're wrong! Yes, I am impassioned every time something

goes awry, but only because in France things seem to be
particularly complicated when it comes to money, business,
commercial dealings. Nothing's easy! A case in point: This
summer I was at a Target store (or, as the French say, *Tar Zhay*) in
Minneapolis where I was erroneously charged for two CDs
when I had purchased only one. I didn't see the error until I was
going over bills with my son in Chicago. I called a suburban
Target to see if we could straighten out the problem (the error was
thirteen dollars, not a major sum, but worth checking out anyway).
No problem: All I had to do was show up at a Target near my
sister's home on the North Shore, show my receipt, and
I would get my money back, no questions asked. I tried to
imagine the same thing happening at a department store in
Marseilles and my getting my money back this simply in
another French town. I just couldn't. France is the
fourth-economic power in the world, but in terms of
customer satisfaction, there's a long way to go.

The idea that the customer is a second-class citizen is so
deeply ingrained that even in stores where you are guar-
anteed your money back, you have to go through an
interrogation. A friend recounted the following dia-
logue in a Monoprix (the French equivalent of a Wool-
worth) where she had taken back a pair of gloves she
had purchased. My friend: "I'd like to give you back
these gloves and get the money back, as I found the
gloves I had wanted to replace." Salesgirl: "Why did
you wait so long?" My friend: "Well, as I said, I just

found them, so I don't need these now, you see?" Sales-girl: "Well, you needed them when you bought them." My friend: "I want to talk to your boss." And that was the end of the story. She got the money back.

First there is the issue of the salesperson's attitude to the customer; then there is the matter of the colossal amount of time wasted because of this attitude. French people have the same experience as Americans do with incompetence and get just as upset by it, if not more. They will also ask themselves why, in a country where streamlined trains run on time, public parks are beautifully kept and safe, and perfection shines in so many realms, one has to put up with the service problem.

I started thinking about this problem seriously during one particularly frustrating week in June in which I had to deal with a magazine subscription my son never received (it was a Christmas gift), as well as threats from a fax manufacturer who said we hadn't paid him for our fax machine. We had, but the company obviously couldn't find a record of the payment. However, they kept sending us menacing letters until they found their mistake, and then they never apologized. The week also included three futile trips to the train station to buy a ticket at a reduced price. It was never to happen, because each time I went, I was told that it wasn't the right day and I would have to come back.

In the same week, my French sister-in-law went absolutely nuts after ordering a refrigerator that, when it arrived, didn't fit into her kitchen. She reordered and the deliverymen came back with another fridge, which again didn't fit. The third time was not the charm, and she is currently hesitating between jumping out of her eleventh-floor window and suing them (the latter is a joke; lawsuits for incompetence are rare in France).

Computers are another major area for problems with price and service. After his last trip to France, my friend Ron Rosbottom, a French professor at Amherst and a bona fide Francophile, recounted: "The French have still not developed a culture of help for the consumer. We may complain in this country that service is going down the tubes, but they haven't even invented it yet, except in cheese shops and restaurants. The French pay a fortune for electronics, but when they break, the seller gives one of those Gallic shrugs that's a cross between 'It's not my problem' and 'A competent person wouldn't have done this.' "

I couldn't have said it better myself.

The question is, Why are commercial dealings so extraordinarily complicated and byzantine?

One explanation is that many times salespeople go too fast and don't listen. If money is dirty, then, by extension, everything concerned with money is dirty. Therefore, it's not healthy to be too interested in the details of any money transaction, and this includes such things as service. (This is my amateur Freudian explanation, but I like it.)

I have often noticed that when salespeople take your order, they want it quickly. If you slow down and explain carefully—but to them, tediously—they rush you along. They just want to move on. Hence the errors resulting from people doing things too fast.

Another explanation is that France is a "high-context" society in which information is supposed to be known but not shared. You are insulting someone if you launch into a laborious explanation. I tried it one day on a salesperson whose eyes literally became glazed with boredom.

Then there is the anonymity. In France, you don't get somebody sitting there with a nameplate reading PAULINE DUPONT. You often find yourself dealing with different people each time there is a transaction. Hence, my son's magazine subscription, where we talked with at least ten different people from the beginning of the unresolved affair to its end. They were all perfectly pleasant, and totally incapable of coming up with a solution until, as often happens in France, I got the director on the case. It was solved immediately.

At the train station, I furiously asked the name of the person in charge. "Just write to the station chief," the man behind the computer console told me. "He doesn't have a name?" I queried incredulously, knowing I would never get it in any case. This ability to hide behind anonymity makes people perfectly irresponsible, and you, the customer, end up paying for their errors.

In line with this is the personalization of the salesperson-client relationship. There is none of this "Business is business—I'll serve anyone who will give me his money" attitude. It is much more a question of "Do I like her face?" If you're on the right side of this equation, this has its distinct advantages.

One cold winter morning, I was going to give a class way out in the southern Paris suburb of Massy Palaiseau. As I was driving along, my little vehicle began stopping, to the tune of honks and gesticulations from the people behind me. After a few more stops and starts, I managed to get off the road and made a beeline for the nearest garage. In the first garage, I asked for the owner, who came out, diagnosed the problem, told me he couldn't help, and directed me to a neighboring garage. There I found a young mechanic to whom I explained that I was on the way to a class and was probably going to lose my job if I didn't show up, and couldn't he please do something for me?

Was it the sincerity of my tone? Was it my American accent? Was it that I was putting my destiny into his hands? Whatever it was, he instantly took an interest in my case, jumped in a truck to go find the parts he didn't have on hand, rushed back within five minutes, installed the broken piece of machinery, and had me ready to go in record time.

The point is that if you can get someone personally interested in your predicament, you will often get amazing results. No one had scheduled me into that mechanic's day, but he took off the time to do my job because he got involved in it. It even became a matter of honor for him to get my car repaired fast and get me on my way.

And while we're on the subject, I can report that I just got back from an exhausting stint of Christmas shopping. Every single salesperson I met was charming, amiable, courteous, wrapping my gifts with the utmost ease and taste. (The whole thing was expensive as all get-out, but that's a fact of life in France; you finally get used to it and bid your hard-earned money good-bye with nary a thought.) It's easy to focus on the negative, but the positive also exists, and as usual, when things go well in France, they go exquisitely well (which is why I have a theory of "magic days" that can only happen in France).

The deal is, I realized, that in France standardized sales behavior does not exist. This results in highly unpredictable situations, but I can think of one distinct advantage. You don't get the "Hi, my name is Joan and I'll be your waitress for the evening" treatment. You may have an adorable waiter (I've had many more professional, well-trained, pleasant waiters than the opposite), a snotty waiter, or something between the two, but at least he'll be himself.

So now that I have figured all this out, I know that

all I need to do is count my change in every store on the street where I live, inure myself to the idea that the customer is *not* always right, and, last but not least, remember never, but never, to *talk* about money. It's dirty, you know.

Interview with Philippe

HARRIET: *French people are always saying that Americans are materialistic. What does that mean? Why don't the French think that they're materialistic?*

PHILIPPE: *The difference is that in France, it's vulgar to talk about money. Talking about money is much worse than talking about sex.*

HARRIET: *As a Frenchman, doesn't it irritate you to be prey to the petty cheating of little shopkeepers? How can you explain this cheating on a small scale?*

PHILIPPE: *You're American. For them, you're supposed to be rich.*

HARRIET: *How about you? You're French, and I've seen you get the same treatment.*

PHILIPPE: *You just yell. That's the end of it.*

HARRIET: *So that doesn't shock you?*

PHILIPPE: *Shopkeepers are made to steal from other people. Otherwise, they would be professors of ancient Sanskrit at the Sorbonne.*

HARRIET: *Oh Lord, the caste system . . . okay, why do people cheat on their taxes?*

PHILIPPE: *Screwing the state doesn't count.*

The Parisians

After attacking (some might say literally) the subjects of food,
sex, the Frenchwoman, and French attitudes toward money, how
about a subject that fascinates everyone who visits Paris: the
Parisians. The five subjects have one thing in common:
They're all hard for a foreigner to figure out.

It was one of those wonderful Parisian evenings when
the air is soft and it's perfect to sit outside on the terrace
of a restaurant and watch the world go by. My husband
and I and an American friend of ours were savoring the
food and the evening when suddenly my husband, irri-
tated by a fox terrier who was getting too close for
comfort, turned to its owner and, wearing his most dis-
agreeable expression, ordered her, "Take your dog and

put him as far away from me as you can." Answer of
dog owner: "You could ask in a nicer tone of voice."
My husband: "I'm not nice." The dog owner: "*Grossier
personnage*" (this is a standard insult, which means
something like "boor" or "vulgar person").

I don't like them, but I'm used to these little restaurant scenes (there are so many dogs in restaurants that
it's hard to avoid a clash). Nonetheless, I could see that
our friend was getting a bit embarrassed. "Would you
see a scene like this in the States?" my husband asked
him, much more relaxed once he had bawled the lady
out and the dog was no longer a problem. "No," replied
our friend. "First of all, you wouldn't see a dog in a restaurant and, second of all, you'd probably get a knife
pulled on you the way you were talking to her."

My husband, a true Parisian, was perfectly satisfied,
even delighted. He had attained his goal, which was to
get rid of the dumb dog which was ruining his dinner.
He didn't care if the dog's owner hated him.

"Welcome to Paris," I told my friend.

As a WASP, and a Midwesterner to boot, I view
fights as things to be avoided. What I realized after two
decades of living with my French husband is that for
a Parisian, a day is no fun if there's no dispute. There
would be nothing to talk about over the dinner table
at night. If you have a knock-down-drag-out with
someone—another driver, a salesperson—you have fuel
for a story in which you emerge the victor and the au-

dience is wowed. This has been going on since the Gauls in Caesar's time; it's really nothing new. (Surely, French writer Jean Cocteau was thinking of a Parisian when he described a Frenchman as "an Italian in a bad mood.")

There's no lack of occasions for getting into arguments in Paris. Dogs are high on the list, either because they have pooped in your path, or because they are going to poop in your path, or because they are licking your leg as you try to digest a meal. On the other hand, a dog can be a man or woman's best pal in Paris. One woman told me that her world changed the day she bought her fox terrier. Before, she had been invisible, even with her two young children in tow. With the dog, people stopped her in the streets, asked her what kind it was, how old it was, told her how cute it was. (They ignored her kids.)

Parisians may be slobs when it comes to letting their dogs poop all over the pavement, but, paradoxically, they are very interested in the cleanliness of their city, forking out one thousand dollars per head per year for it. Hence, some six thousand city employees clean the city in one way or another twenty-four hours a day. And, a friend told me, this includes Christmas Day, when she was astonished to hear the clatter of the garbage truck.

Many quarrels, I have noticed, revolve around the car, one of the primary reasons for the bad humor of

Parisians. Before I started driving, I thought of Paris as an almost gentle place to live, a place of radiant beauty. I walked on a cloud, with my head in the air, admiring centuries-old buildings and penthouse apartments (not a good idea, I found, after slipping in dog doo). After I got up the nerve to drive, though, I discovered a whole new world, and all the various possibilities for disputes arising from the possession of a vehicle. Paris must be a lovely place to live in if you have a chauffeur.

Of course, a real Parisian, like my husband, thrives on the thrill of driving in Paris. He heads into the no-lane traffic mess around the Arc de Triomphe with glee. Whenever I can, I avoid the "Circle from Hell." When I can't, well, I've learned to fend for myself and actually enjoy watching the Parisians as they both drive *and* chat on car phones, file their nails, smoke big fat cigars, and flirt with one another. Why not?

I discovered that, among other things, there seems to be an unwritten rule stating that a Parisian puts his car where he wants to when he wants to. It can block a garage or another car or an entry reserved for ambulances. None of these obstacles pose a problem for the Parisian. On one typical morning, my husband discovered that his car was blocked by an inconsiderate soul who had double-parked his van, locked the doors, and totally vanished. What can one do? My husband got his revenge by taking out a tube of greasy lipstick (which he keeps with him for this purpose) and scrawling something unprintable on the person's windshield. He then proceeded to go to work . . . on the Métro.

As I live in a neighborhood of nouveaux riches, this means that not only do the people have all the Parisian characteristics of aggressivity and hostility and general impoliteness but, on top of that, since they are newly rich, they think that anything worth having can be bought. Manners not being a commodity, there's no reason to have any!

On one rainy day shortly before Christmas, an elderly lady in our building went out to get into her red Renault 5 but couldn't leave because she was blocked by another car. That's par for the course around here, but infuriating all the same. After a good half hour, she finally spied the offender coming toward her. I thought in my naïveté that the guilty party would profusely apologize. Wrong. This made my neighbor even more furious. So she hauled off and belted the culprit. You may think this is the end of the story and that they were even. No!

The Hateful Guilty One grabbed one of my neighbor's windshield wipers, ripped it out, and yelled, "That'll teach you to lay your hands on me!" (Remember, all this is taking place in a neighborhood that is the French equivalent of Westchester, Winnetka, or Knightsbridge.) She then trounced off to the astonishment of the little group that by this time had gathered around to witness the brawl. But she didn't get far. A gallant Frenchman, yelling and shouting, dashed to the car of the offender as she was about to drive off . . . and gave a healthy kick to her rear lights, breaking them.

These kinds of incidents happen *often*.

There seems to be another unwritten rule among Parisians: Always get even with the appropriate response. By that, I mean something rather elegant that you just throw off, such as *"Je vous emmerde, madame!"* *("F - - - you, madam.")* Even when they are rude, even when they are driving, the French stick to form.

Getting your car into a parking place is also fun and games. In Paris, the method is to bang the car in back of you and then bang the one in front as you maneuver in (or out). If you're lucky, the driver of one or the other will have left his emergency brake off, which facilitates the easing in or out. I tried this in the States. Unfortunately for me, the owner of the car I bumped into was standing right in front of his Chinese restaurant. I thought I was going to end up as chop suey. In France, everyone yells and screams and gesticulates and threatens, but you never FEAR FOR YOUR LIFE OR THINK YOU'LL END UP WITH A BULLET IN YOU. I surmised from the reactions of my fellow Americans that we need some lessons in Parisian creative driving.

Creative driving means that if all of a sudden you decide to turn around in the middle of a road, you just do it. Creative driving means that you go as fast as you can to get to the red light, where you'll be stopped anyway. The point is to get to the red light *faster.* There are some French drivers who don't even bother to stop at red lights. Anyway, the purpose of driving for all these Cyranos is not just to get from point A to point B, but to do it with panache, style. The quality of the driving seems to be inversely proportional to the size of the car, the worst drivers being in the smallest cars, the Renault 5s and the Peugeot 205s. Do French cars also have a Napoléon complex?

Anyway, not to worry. You get used to all of this. Besides, there are a few advantages to this strange, hectic behavior. No cop will ever pick you up for crossing the street against a red light—France must be the only place on earth where the meter maids jaywalk.

A friend of mine pointed out that I seem to be a bit obsessed about cars. She's right and I am! I mean, imagine having a car and parking it in a street in Paris because you don't have a garage. Then imagine an assorted group of pigeons all flying above it and doing you know what to it. Next, imagine rows of beautiful linden trees dripping their sap over said car on top of the pigeon excrement. Finally, imagine people regularly bumping into it as they park—once in front and once in back—when they're not hemming it in so you can't even get it to the nearest car wash! Do you become obsessed? *Un peu, oui!*

Although I quickly adjusted to driving and parking, I had a much harder time grasping the Parisian concept of a *line*. I finally figured out that a Parisian queue doesn't look like one because it is not an orderly formation, but, rather, a collection of motley individuals all trying to get in front of one another.

You always have to be sure to ask where the end of the line is in order to ascertain that you are in the right place. The next step is to make sure that no one jumps ahead of you. This happens all the time, so you have to be on the alert constantly. If you're a real Parisian, the minute there's a suspect move, you start yelling. If you're a foreigner, even one who's been here a long time, as I have, you tend to wait a bit, not wanting to believe that that person wants to get your place.

In the market, at the bakery, but especially at the post office and banks, where you can easily fossilize if you don't catch on to the great game of queue hopping, you must concentrate all your forces on defending your place in line. At the market, when the vendor yells, "Whose turn is it?" you'd better be ready to yell "*moi.*" Heaven help you if you've goofed and it's not really your turn. Every time I go to the market, I am a nervous wreck for a half hour afterward from the strain of making sure no one is going to slip by and take my place or from the strain of not having slugged the person behind me, who is pushing me.

The Silent Pusher is an endemic Parisian phenomenon. He or she is generally someone who is unhappy about not being in front of you but is afraid to tell you so directly.

You will be standing in line waiting for a movie, say, and feel someone jostling you. You turn around and see nothing special happening. You go back to reading your newspaper or talking to your friends and then feel it again. The Silent Pusher is hard to catch. One day, my family stood in line for a movie in Montparnasse. All the while we were standing, I was being elbowed but couldn't catch the offender. When we got inside, my son turned to me and said, "That lady behind me was pushing me the whole time!" "Oh, you, too!" I laughed, vowing that the next time I would spray a few cans of tear gas to make some space for myself and my family.

The only place I have seen Parisians almost refrain from this pushing and shoving was at Euro Disneyland. On the contrary, I never dreamed the French could be so positively disciplined as they patiently waited forty-five minutes for the three-minute ride down Big Thunder Mountain. Of course it is to Disney's credit that we were literally corralled into the Big Thunder Mine and there was no way, even for the enterprising French, to cut into or get out of line.

Then there's the post office. One day I had one hundred letters to post to the States. There was nary a soul in line, but the girl behind the counter informed me that I would be holding up a *potential* line if she were to pass each letter through her machine and that the only solution would be for me to lick each stamp individually. I honestly think that ten years ago I would have licked every single stamp, but fortunately I have outgrown that. Imitating a real Parisian, I haughtily told her that I would like to speak to her *"directeur."* She passed the letters through the machine.

Another Parisian idiosyncracy can be found in speech. First of all, Parisians speak faster than Frenchmen elsewhere. Second of all, they never really mean what they say or say what they mean. French journalist Alain Schifres points out in his book *Les Parisiens (The Parisians)* that, for example, if a Parisian says that something is *pas mal* (not bad), that means it is pretty good and certainly better than if he said *moyen* (average).

If, Schifres continues, a Parisian says that his son or daughter is a cretin or somehow mentally defective (the French haven't discovered PC yet; you can still say things like that here), it means he is very proud of him or her! My husband, a typical Parisian, indulges in this Paris-speak rather often. To hear him tell it, his three sons will be lucky if they end up as garbage collectors, when in reality the firstborn is a doctor, the second made it into a prestigious grande école, and the third is on the path to fame and glory (hey, somebody around here has to brag).

Other hidden codes, according to Schifres, who has been around Parisian circles long enough to detect these nuances, are expressions like *"Il est mignon"* which does not mean he is cute, the literal translation, but rather "he is naïve." If someone says of another person that he is conscientious, it actually means that he is an imbecile. The worst is "Everybody likes him a lot," which, translated from Parisian vernacular, means "He's a failure."

Parisians also have favorite subjects. One of these, which has become less so since the bottom fell out of the market, is real estate. The conversation generally revolves around how much apartments have gained in value ("I could never buy this now") or how expensive rents are.

Real estate terms are a prime example of Paris-speak. An American relocation specialist and friend one day explained the hidden meaning of certain real estate terms, starting with the word *coquet*. Basically, to describe an apartment as *coquet* (adorable) is to say it's so small a midget couldn't stand up in it. The words *standing* (pronounced *stawndeeng*) and *grand standing* simply mean that the apartment referred to is not low-income housing. *Standing* usually refers to an apartment in a 1960s building with fake stone blocks, paper-thin walls, and a thin coat of grease in the kitchen. An apartment with *standing* generally needs a troop of cleaners to get off the grime, says my friend. An apartment qualified as having *grand standing* is usually done up with glass and chrome and so many marble floors that you feel as if you're walking on kitchen counters or are in a showroom for tombstones.

Mignon (cute) is better than *coquet* because you can

stand up straight, but of course you can touch both walls with your elbows. When an ad says "*grenier amé-nageable,*" indicating that there's an attic that can be fixed up, it means you'll need to redo the roof. And when the ad mentions that the apartment just needs "refreshing" with a little "*coup de peinture*" (paint job), it means that the whole thing needs to be completely and totally refurbished, including replastering the walls and maybe redoing the electricity.

Having always rented apartments, I can affirm that when the French say "unfurnished," it means the place has been stripped down to lightbulblessness. When we moved into our current apartment, the kitchen was so "unfurnished" that there was nothing but the kitchen sink—and I was amazed to find even that! Under French law, the owner is not required to paint the place he rents. This, along with the price of painters, may explain why so many beautiful apartments are run-down. The lowest estimate to get my thirty-five-square-meter living room painted was eight thousand francs (about $1,300), and that was off the books and considered a steal. The highest estimate for the same room was 100,000 francs (about $16,500). It's still not painted.

It seems like the Japanese have a particularly hard time understanding Parisian behavior.

The behavior of the Parisians may sometimes be incomprehensible to an American like me who has lived here for over twenty years, but it is almost a total mystery to some nationalities. Although one million Japanese flock to France each year and approximately 25,000 live in Paris, it would be an understatement to say that the Japanese have a hard time penetrating the French psyche.

Many Japanese have such a hard time adjusting to life in the French capital that one Japanese psychiatrist, married to a Frenchwoman, has baptized the phenomenon "Paris stress." Doctor Hiroaki Ota, the head of the Association Franco-Japonaise de Psychiatrie et Sciences Humaines (Franco-Japanese Association of Psychiatry and Social Sciences), explains that this is not a malady, strictly speaking, but "a perturbed psychological state accompanied by indeterminate somatic symptoms such as irritability, a feeling of fear, obsession, depressed mood, insomnia, impression of persecution by the French."

This would sound almost funny if it weren't a very serious problem. Dr. Ota, who since 1987 has specialized in consultations for members of the Japanese community at the renowned Saint Anne psychiatric hospital in Paris, has a private clientele of 715 patients, and of them, three times as many women as men. His patients are divided into three categories: businessmen working for Japanese companies and in Paris with their families, Japanese or Franco-Japanese residents of Paris, and tourists. Some of these are "light" cases, which can be dealt with in ten to twenty counseling sessions. Others are more serious and take longer.

One of the main problems for some of the Japanese businessmen is that they have jumped from one work category to another. They may have worked in nonprofessional jobs in Japan, but to be able to come to France, they have to qualify for "professional" (or, as the French say, "*cadre*") positions to get a work permit. This means that they are asked to make decisions and carry out work that they are absolutely not used to doing in Japan, and all this in a foreign language. Under the strain of it, many become depressive.

The cultural shock for the Japanese is not just the language, but everything that goes with the language, all the nuances, the nonverbal talk. One thing that particularly mystifies the Japanese, as it does other nationalities, is how fast the Parisians talk and how often they interrupt one another's conversations. French humor, which consists largely of poking fun at other people, is no fun for the Japanese because they are unable to respond with alacrity. According to Dr. Ota, "They can't decipher the different levels of the meaning of a discourse and stop at the first level, which, in French humor, often contains aggressive or vexing elements." (Americans as well often stop at the "first level," even though in France, it's better to probe more deeply into what is being said, because it's not always what is on the surface.)

Another hard thing for the Japanese to cope with,

Dr. Ota tells me, is the changing moods of the French, who are given to blowing up suddenly and calming down just as quickly. A Japanese thinks, It's because of me that that person is angry, and he feels guilty. The Japanese take into account the emotions of the person or persons they are addressing, whereas the French base their discussions on logic and rationality. Dr. Ota says he advises his patients, those who are only light cases, to confront French reality by observing the French but not trying to "move with them." In Japan, he says, life is more structured, calmer, more disciplined, and the discipline is respected. "In France things appear to be without discipline, but there is one."

One situation Japanese businessmen in particular have trouble coping with is the business meeting *(la réunion)*. "In Japan we have a meeting once something is almost decided, and the meeting is just to confirm and conclude. In France, everyone is talking all at once and they are too tired to accomplish anything." For the French, "principles are very important, which is why the French are such good diplomats," says Ota. "For the Japanese, pragmatism is what counts."

Talking in general is a problem. For the Japanese, as for Anglo-Saxons, the spoken word is important, serious. "The French talk as if they are strolling. The conversation doesn't go anywhere," says Ota. And this leads to confusion for the Japanese, who have trouble, in any case, formulating an answer before the French have skipped to another subject. And yet, "if you don't talk here, you don't exist," another contradiction for the Japanese, for whom silence and discretion are important.

The Japanese aren't alone in not understanding the French (and the Parisians in particular). The English have a centuries-old love-hate relationship with the French, which regularly springs up in the English tabloid press in the form of "hate Froggy" insults. The Americans—well, as one who has lived here for over two decades, I can attest to the fact that the Parisians, including my husband, are not always the world's easiest people to understand. And yet—this is the crux—one is never bored!

If there are so many cultural differences and the French are so cryptic, why, one might ask, do so many people keep coming—and staying? To which my Parisian husband would reply, "Where else in the world could you live?" As one Paris-lover remarked a century ago, "I only know that I found in Paris all and even more than I was expecting. I only know that I was charmed and enchanted more than I can say."

In 1869, Mark Twain wrote of Paris in *The Innocents Abroad:* "We secured rooms at the hotel, or rather, we had three beds put into one room, so that we might be together, and then we went out to a restaurant, just after lamplighting, and ate a comfortable, satisfactory, lingering dinner. It was a pleasure to eat where everything was so tidy, the food so well cooked, the waiters so polite, and the coming and departing company so moustached, so frisky, so affable, so fearfully and wonderfully Frenchy!"

But the tribute I love the best is one written by Joe Murray in an "Opinion" column in the *International Herald Tribune:* "Paris should be declared an international shrine. The World Bank should finance its economy. The people of Paris should work at no other job than simply that of being Parisians."

I can only wholeheartedly agree with Joe Murray and Mark Twain. It surely must be this "fearfully and wonderfully Frenchy" side that's kept me here for all these years, and I must confess (now I mustn't get sentimental here) that I find this city as beautiful as the first day I laid eyes on it. Even with all the incomprehensible cultural differences and a certain amount of moaning and groaning about the inevitable vicissitudes of city life, I can't really imagine where else I could possibly live. I guess I've become a real *Parisienne* after all.

Interview with Philippe

HARRIET: *After all I have written here, do you have the feeling that I am being unfair, or even racist, about Parisians?*

PHILIPPE: *Absolutely! Paris is not just taxi drivers or surly waiters. The criminality has nothing to do with what you find in the States. It's better to get a* coup de pare-chocs *than a* coup de revolver *[a bang in the fender than a bang from a gun]. Parisians may be obnoxious but you can still drive around here without locking all your windows and doors.*

HARRIET: *How about dog poop and snarling sales-people? What do you have to say about that?*

PHILIPPE: *Shoot them all.*

HARRIET: *Okay, one more question. Why do the Parisians do everything so fast?*

PHILIPPE: *Because they're—we're—agitated.* Voilà. *And only a person from Iowa could live here for over twenty years and maintain* your *rhythm.*

HARRIET: *I've often noticed that Parisians make fun not only of foreign accents but even of French accents that are not Parisian. How do you Parisians situate yourselves in relationship to other Frenchmen?*

PHILIPPE: *What other Frenchmen?*

Politesse

It may be hard to figure out why the French, and especially the Parisians, act as they do, but if you're a tourist, you probably don't really care. However, if you live in France, there are a few things you have to try to understand, such as French rules of politesse, which are so complicated that they take years to grasp. Only then do you realize all the gaffes and mistakes you've been making!

As the years passed, I made an amazing discovery that enabled me to understand why the French have such a worldwide reputation for rudeness. In France, you are not expected to like everybody or even act as if you do.

The good side of this is that your smile muscles don't get worn out, because you rarely use them; the bad side is that since the French in general reserve their true sentiments and warmth for the people they know, many foreigners come away thinking that the French are universally impolite. They can rest assured. The French treat one another even worse than they treat foreigners.

It's true that there's no premium placed on being nice to people you don't know. Inconsiderate acts such as double-parking the car, taking dogs to restaurants, or smoking in elevators are all perpetrated on people you don't know and hence don't care about. Relieving oneself by the side of a road or major thoroughfare falls into the same category, but with a little macho tinge.

On the other hand, the French have a set of codes for polite behavior that is extremely complicated. I know now, for example, that I have made many gaffes by being too candid. In France, for instance, there is no intrinsic merit in being frank and to the point.

Au contraire. The blunt way we Americans say things is considered by polite French people to be "violent" (the word they use for it in French is the same—*violent*). Even if a statement is true, the French won't appreciate it coming at them in a strong-arm fashion. The oblique is better than the direct. Wrap up your comment in a pretty package and deliver it to your listener on a platter. You're on your way.

Try this exercise in politesse: Your neighbor's radio is driving you nuts and you want to do something about it. As an American, I would go to the person and say, "Could you please turn your radio down?" A French person with manners would phrase it differently. "Have you moved your radio? I never used to hear it before." The person, if he or she is French, will get the hint.

I decided to test my level of subtlety the day my new neighbor asked me if I would like her to put up a divider so that I wouldn't see all her washing hanging out on the back porch we share. I hypocritically said, "No, it doesn't bother me," a bold-faced lie. I delightedly reported the incident to my husband, noting that for once in my life, I had been indirect. "No," my husband told me, "you got it all wrong." A French person would have put the ball in her court: "It's up to you. I don't know whether you mind other people seeing your personal belongings." Translation: "Of course I don't want to look out my kitchen window at your underwear, you sap!"

In the heart of the country, at the home of some people we didn't know, we were offered an aperitif. Unfortunately, a fly landed in my drink. Without my ever seeing it, my husband quickly exchanged glasses, all the while talking to the host. I never knew what he did with the fly—I think he plucked it out and flicked it into the fireplace. In any event, no one ever knew what happened, including me, and that was only because he told me afterward. Calling attention to the fly, as I surely would have done, would have been totally un-thinkable.

In line with this, the phone is another battlefield for cultural differences. When my American friends call, I say, "May I call you back? I'm eating." My husband says that is the height of rudeness. He himself would pick up the phone and let his food go cold rather than cut someone off. For him, telling the caller that you are otherwise engaged means that you have better things to do than talk to him, and it puts the person in the awkward position of having to apologize.

When I counter that my friends would be embarrassed to have me on the phone an hour if they knew I was eating, he doesn't understand. (I have on many occasions called my sister-in-law, and the only indication that she had company was that she would say, "Oh, no problem, we're just going to the table." Translation: "I'm busy!") Raymonde Carroll explains in *Cultural Misunderstandings* that phoning for the French is a ritual and that "picking up the telephone to tell a friend ready for ritual that one is not free to participate constitutes an incongruity for a French person."

In another sterling paradox, while the French can be monumentally impolite when they want to be, at the same time they are almost Japanese in their way of circumventing delicate situations so that the other person can be spared discomfiture or can save face. A telling scene: A friend was accosted by a driver who almost mowed her down to get a parking place he thought she had stolen from him. It turned out that the same night she was invited to a party and introduced to an exquisite young man with lovely manners. When she looked him full in the face, she discovered, to her consternation, that he was the mad driver. She didn't know whether he recognized her or not. In a typical bourgeois ballet, each pretended never to have seen the other.

By the same token, the French often speak in double negatives to avoid unpleasant situations. It is a great way to hedge. Saying, "I wouldn't say no," or "I'm not unhappy," or "It's not bad" instead of "Yes" or "Great!" is a way of not exposing yourself to ridicule and/or of reserving your judgment. My husband talks this way all the time. One day, however, we got into an elevator and in a friendly way he said to the person we were riding with, "That exhibition was great, wasn't it?" and the stranger answered, "No!" Guess who looked stupid, and the French *hate* looking stupid.

As if this verbal juggling is not enough, the French have codes and secret signs that only they can figure out. These codes, which they recognize but no one else does, can cause incredible misunderstandings. For years, my American family and many non-French friends thought my husband was a real check-grabber. What they didn't realize was that he would lunge for the bill forcefully, quite confident that there would be an instantaneous remonstrance and he wouldn't end up with it. The problem was that with non-French people, he only succeeded in scaring them into thinking that he really did want to pay, and they let him!

"Why do you keep doing that?" I would ask him. He explained to me that French people would understand right away that his gesture was one of politeness, an offer that was not necessarily to be taken up. I explained to him that Americans take people literally, so no wonder he got stuck in such predicaments. Once he figured out this was yet another enormous cultural gap, he changed his behavior—fortunately, before we went bankrupt.

Codes are hard to decipher. As Edward and Mildred Hall point out in *Understanding Cultural Differences*, Americans "are often uncomfortable with indirectness and sometimes miss nonverbal cues: subtle shifts in voice, slight, almost imperceptible changes in body posture or breathing." I know I certainly miss a lot, including with one Frenchman, who happens to be my husband. He's always sending me very subtle brain waves I absolutely don't get.

To leave a dinner party, instead of turning to our hosts and saying, "Well, it's really been fun, but it's late and time to go," he starts staring at me very hard. When I don't get that, he resorts to his pained look, mouth curved down at the corners. All the while, I am laughing it up. When we finally leave, he says, "It's so late. Didn't you see me telling you it was time to go?"

I stare at him, astonished. "Why didn't you just say 'It's time to go'?" I ask him.

"Because you're supposed to see my signal," he replies.

We will never get together on this particular cultural divide.

The need for delicacy and privacy is seen in the fact that the French don't really appreciate personal questions such as "What do you do?" or, worse, "Where do you work?" Even such a seemingly innocent question as "What does your father do?" is best avoided. Why? Because the person might come from a lower-class family and have a high-level job—or come from an aristocratic family and have a low-level job. This is changing now, but it is safe to say that you can have a ten-hour conversation with a French person and never know his name, job, or personal status. Try to do that in the States.

Americans, generally speaking, are just looking for information and couldn't care less if a person's family is composed of nobles or cobblers. Hence, we have a hard time coping with the twists and turns of roundabout conversations. But the French are constantly aware of social hierarchy, the place they occupy in society, whether it be their job or their social class. A French friend explained the difference to me this way: "Politeness is avoiding asking a question that will put the person in a position that could show either that he is wrong or criticizable. You have to think of the difficulty he may have in giving an answer." So much for direct questions.

The complications involved in avoiding direct references to your profession or employer can result in curious situations. A new acquaintance told us, without ever naming the firm, that he worked for a huge public company employing thousands of people doing very special kinds of projects in the field of housing and transportation. About five minutes into this byzantine description, my husband named a company and said, "You wouldn't happen to work there, would you?" And they both laughed, as the company turned out to be the one my husband works for, as well.

Anglo-Saxons feel they have to proffer their names if they're going to sustain a conversation lasting any longer than five minutes. They also feel the need to introduce people who don't know one another, even if they can't remember the people's names. The French are just the opposite. I have been going to a gym class near my home for the past four years. The women are perfectly friendly for the most part, but I don't know the name of any of the women I stand and sweat next to. We exchange smiles and even conversations, but not *names*. Another example: At a luncheon, I sat next to a charming mother and daughter with whom I conversed for approximately five hours. Never once did we exchange names!

A young American told me of his astonishment at not being remarked upon or included when he found himself in a group of people he didn't know: "When you go to a party in the States and you're the newcomer, everyone would want to know your name, what you do, where you are from—but in France, I can't tell you the number of parties I have been to where I am the only American in a group of close-knit friends and no one says anything to me. The guy who invites you doesn't even say, 'This is Dave' to the others. If the guy next to you is outgoing, you'll get questions, but if you are shy, you're out of luck. As soon as *I* ask questions, it breaks the ice." You will note that he said "as soon as *I* ask questions"—the burden is on the newcomer.

While taking a walk in the park one Sunday, we saw someone my husband works with every day. He was with his wife and children, both of whom we knew. Accompanying them was an older woman, whom I presumed was the mother of one of them, but I'll never know, because no one ever introduced us. We just stood there and chatted and then left. My husband's comment: "Thank God we didn't get into introductions. I have no desire to know his relatives, and I'm sure he feels the same about mine!"

One good thing about this formality is that you don't have to invite the boss to dinner: The French Revolution was supposed to usher in an age of equality, but don't ever go so far as to think that the French forget their sense of hierarchy. You may be invited to dinner by your husband's boss, or your husband may invite his secretary to dinner, but the subordinate is not expected to repay the invitation: In fact, it just wouldn't do. The higher-up can in this way exercise his power of noblesse oblige. The underling is supposed to stay in his proper place. An invitation from the subordinate would put his hierarchical superior in a disadvantageous situation, forcing him to "come down." In addition, the underling might feel apologetic for not having a big-enough house or nice-enough furniture. Fortunately for both parties, the rules are clear, so no one has to worry about it.

There is one occasion, however, when naming names becomes vital. When invited to someone's home, you're not to show up with a friend; you're to ask permission and then give the name. I knew the part about asking permission to invite a friend, of course, but I had to be told that the name part is very important. In this land of complicated professional and private relationships, it is essential to provide the names when asking permission to take an extra guest to a party. Who knows, you may have inadvertently invited someone's mistress!

It would seem that there are a series of written and unwritten rules for just about everything. Take a breeze, for example. The French call it a *courant d'air* (draft) and, in my French family at least, flee it like the pest, believing perhaps that it will bring the plague. The first time I opened doors to let in a breeze, my in-laws rushed around feverishly shutting them, fearing perhaps that I was letting in an evil spirit, or worse. I now save my breezes for when I am alone. Perhaps for this reason, when you are on a bus or train and there is a discussion about whether the window should be opened or closed, the person who wants it closed will always win.

Then there's the dinner party. In my early days here, I didn't know the following:

When French people invite you at a certain hour, you should add fifteen or twenty minutes to that time. If you arrive right on time, not only will you be the first but chances are things may not be ready. The announced time is the first possible time at which you could arrive, but not the time the host really expects you or hopes to see you.

You are not to show up—ever—with a bouquet of chrysanthemums, flowers the French reserve for cemeteries, or carnations, which are considered bad luck! In fact, if you're a supersophisticate, you either send flowers before, giving the hostess time to arrange them, or send them after the dinner with a thank-you note. The French being proud of their logic, the Cartesian point here is that it is awkward for the hostess to have to run around finding the right-size vase. Also, if you have brought an especially grand bouquet, it might embarrass other guests, whose offerings pale in comparison. *C'est logique.*

You won't be shown around the house. Once again, the French like to keep what's private . . . private.

In a dinner party situation, it's vital to keep in mind everything I've said earlier about noise levels. Don't talk or laugh too loudly. Avoid frank outbursts. In terms of wine, they drink enough to enjoy it, but not enough to get plastered and make fools of themselves. "Use, do not abuse: neither abstinence nor excess ever renders man happy," wrote Voltaire.

It all boils down to the observance of a state the French admire greatly: moderation. In line with this, it is considered extremely impolite to call attention to oneself. As French journalist Ghislaine Andreani observes in her *Guide du Nouveau Savoir-Vivre (Guide to New Etiquette),* "There are ways to express your joy in life." However, she warns, "Don't guffaw, don't burst out laughing, don't laugh loudly in society, in a restaurant, in the street." Perhaps that explains the withering looks we non-French (and ill-mannered French) often get as we heartily crack up in movies, restaurants, and all sorts of other public places.

It's when you hit the dinner table that the number of mistakes you can make increases considerably. The first thing I learned was that once you get to the table, you shouldn't plan to leave it except in dire stress, and even then, you are to fade away gently. Do not—*quelle horreur*—announce where it is that you might be going.

Then there's the delicate matter of where to put your hands. Elbows on the table? Hands under the table? The rule on this is essentially Latin in spirit. Etiquette decrees that hands should always be on or above the table, lest it seem that any hanky-panky be going on under it.

Eating with one's fingers is another dinner table no-no. The French have perfected the art of eating with a knife and fork. Picking up a chicken leg or a barbecued sparerib with one's fingers is definitely out. That also includes pizza, which is eaten with a knife and fork, not the hands.

I thought that this rule could easily be violated in the company of French-American couples, and so on one occasion where I was being served fried chicken, I asked my American hostess if I could pick it up and eat it with my hands, which in my book is the only way to eat fried chicken. (This, while everyone else was cutting away ever so delicately.) Of course, she assented, not daring to do so herself, because her French husband would have killed her on the spot.

At formal parties, asparagus is always fun to eat. I hear that it is to be decapitated ever so neatly with a knife and fork, and the sauce should be recovered with the fork, as well. On informal occasions, you can actually pick the asparagus up with your fingers and maneuver it around to get the sauce. In both cases, however, you're supposed to eat only the tips.

The French extend the use of knife and fork to fruit. One American friend of mine reports having once seen a woman in a restaurant eating a *banana* with a knife and fork. You have to see it to believe it. And no fair taking the fruit in your hands to cut: Proper etiquette requires that it remain on the plate during this surgical operation.

On the other hand, cutting salad greenery is unforgivable. The knife should be used gently to help fold really big lettuce leaves so that they can be speared with the fork, with the ever-present risk, of course, that a leaf will pop up and unfold just before reaching one's mouth. The tradition of not cutting salad apparently stems from the fact that the acidity of the vinegar used to rust the blade of the knife. This is no longer true, but the custom holds.

While we're on the subject of food, it would appear that soup should always be sipped from the end of the soup spoon, not the side, in direct opposition to Anglo-Saxon etiquette.

When you see a delicious sauce sitting in front of you, you're very tempted to sop it up with the bread. Actually, millions of Frenchmen do—at home—but when invited out, it's a big no-no. Even cheating by skewing a piece of bread on the fork and then swishing it around the plate is bad form. At my mother-in-law's house, I used to do something that no polite person would ever do, which was to take the white out of the bread and just eat the crust (I redden even to tell it). In her Périgourdine dialect, she called these little balls my *tapous*. Well, let me tell you, it didn't take me long to figure out that making *tapous* was taboo.

From the time he learns to chew, every Frenchman is taught that *le pain* is a commodity not to be wasted. Hence, it is generally served already cut and you take only what you intend to eat (a general rule for the rest of the meal, as well). If an entire baguette is put on the table, you break it rather than cut it. Why break rather than cut the baguette? The answer to this is best provided by the Baronne Staffe in her book *Règles du Savoir-Vivre (Rules of Etiquette)*. For the Baronne, it is quite obvious that "pieces could, under the effort of the knife, jump into the eyes of the guests" or, even worse, "on uncovered shoulders." Of course, the Baronne Staffe's little guide was written in 1889, when women dressed (or undressed) for dinner, and perhaps baguettes were crustier than they are now—but the tradition still holds today.

What to do when confronted with French cheese? This is a very unsettling experience the first time around. For people like me from the land of Velveeta, how exciting and frightening to see, all on one plate, a gorgeous blue-veined Roquefort, a whitey-yellow Gruyère, a perfect ash-covered chèvre, a creamy Reblochon. My late father-in-law took particular pride in presenting the cheese plate. Every single time he passed it, he would tell me exactly which cheese was on the plate and then present it as if it were a very special gift. "You must try this," he would say, indicating the *feuille de Dreux,* a regional specialty, or say, "The Brie is particularly good today."

But how does one cut cheese without perpetrating an

atrocity? I learned, after cutting the nose off a Brie and massacring the Roquefort, that this is basically a question of common sense. Gruyère is cut lengthwise, round cheeses in wedges. Roquefort and all blue cheese are cut so that the last person doesn't end up with all the white. Stands to reason. For all but the most calorie-conscious, Roquefort is often eaten with butter, all mashed up. Very bad for the cholesterol, but I refuse to get into that argument, because it would ruin my appetite. If people do choose to indulge in the Roquefort-butter combination, though, they mostly do so in the privacy of their own homes, not when invited out.

Another thing I've learned is that cheese goes around the table only once, and French custom is to never serve coffee with dessert, but after, as a separate course. *Très civilisé.*

Now, if you are in a French home and have had dessert and coffee and after-dinner drinks and the hostess suddenly suggests a nice glass of fruit juice, you know it is time to leave. In the old days, when people had a tendency to consume alcoholic after-dinner drinks, such as Cointreau or cognac, offering fruit juice meant that you had really been around too long. Now that people tend to drink less and especially have reduced their consumption of after-dinner drinks, the fruit juice routine somehow seems less menacing. But it still means the same thing: The party's over.

Finally, the absolutely worst thing you can do in a

French home, at least in my mother-in-law's French home, is not to clean your plate. She explained it to me this way: "If you are serving yourself as the food is passed, you should just take what you are going to eat and eat it *all*. If you leave something, it is an insult to your hostess, who will assume that you didn't like it."

My mother-in-law, it must be said, does not apply the clean-plate rule to restaurants. There, she says, again with correct French logic, you are paying for your meal, so you eat what you want and leave the rest.

Having absorbed the food lesson (no pun intended),
let's now move on to how to give compliments, how to give a *bise*,
and how many to give, how to converse and whether to drop in on
people or not. Elementary, my dear Watson? Not really.

As far as compliments are concerned, they seem to be a source of embarrassment more than anything else. In fact, the direct compliment seems to plunge the recipient into a state of confusion. Writing in the late nineteenth century, the good Baronne Staffe advised her readers that "well-brought up people never give totally direct compliments, because these compliments can embarrass people who are modest, timid, a bit shy, and because it is embarrassing to answer a compliment coming from such close range."

In Anglo-Saxon countries, when someone says something nice, you are taught to say thank you very simply. In France, the situation is much more complicated. At the end of a lovely evening in the home of French friends, I complimented the mother on the wonderful manners of her three boys. "Oh, you know, they're not always like that. When their father's gone, they are positively horrible sometimes," she said, secretly pleased. A friend of mine told me that her daughter, who is half-French and was raised in France, had told her that she liked the way I was dressed. My friend asked her, "Did you tell Harriet?" And the daughter replied, "No, I didn't dare." So the compliment seems to be more problematic than one would think.

When first in France, I would literally groan with delight at what I was served at my mother-in-law's house, until the day I could see that she thought I was making fun of her! For her, an exquisite lettuce salad with a perfect vinaigrette was something she made every day, and so how could it be so extraordinary?

The best way I have of complimenting her now is to ask her for her recipes. However, it is not proper to ask for recipes while at the table, for obvious reasons. Suppose the dinner has been catered? Many hostesses prefer to leave a bit of ambiguity as to the origin of the food. I learned this from my sister-in-law, who is a wonderful cook but who has been known to serve a frozen dish along with freshly prepared when pressed. Rather than publicly confess it, she says absolutely nothing. At the beginning, this bothered me. But I must be becoming French. I now think, Why *should* she tell all? She's the cook!

So, do you compliment the hostess on the food? Some do; some don't. Some etiquette manuals say it is best to reserve a compliment for the dessert, probably to avoid getting into a discussion about food, because, while it's good to eat, there's nothing so boring as to talk about it while consuming it.

Conversation, like many other things, has been elevated to an art form in France and is, even if you speak French well or your hosts speak fluent English, an area loaded with pitfalls. At dinners where people don't know one another, the conversation is expected to be light and never to bog down in personal or "heavy" matters.

I used to sit in amazement and listen to these conversations, which for me were like the sounds of birds in an aviary, all chirping at once. An American friend asked me why conversations at these parties are so superficial and why no one seriously answers you when you ask a question, or why no one listens to your answer when you reply to a question. Serious answers, I told him, are *out*. Why? You might bore your entourage.

As French author André Maurois put it, "The conversation-game is a work of art.... A passionate man always spoils a conversation-game. He seriously refutes light arguments; he follows themes which have been abandoned. The rule is to accept all the movements of the ball and to follow it without regret."

Other than table manners, the art of conversation, and the mysteries of the simple compliment, I found there were other things to learn. It seems that the French are always touching one another, kissing hands, shaking hands, or giving one another pecks on the cheek. There are even rules for all this. For example, the famous *baisemain*. Americans aren't used to this, and one American friend told me that the first time it happened to her, she instinctively snatched her hand away for fear of being bitten! (She needn't have feared a bit—technically, the lips do no more than graze the hand.) Do people really still do that in this day and age? Well, yes, rather more than you might think, depending on the social circle. Nevertheless, the *baisemain* is technically off-limits in the case of unmarried women, women wearing gloves, and women in public places.

There is another rule as well concerning greeting people. For example, when my children were growing up, it seemed to be a matter of great consequence that they say, *"Bonjour, madame"* or *"Bonjour, monsieur,"* as opposed to just a short *"Bonjour."* Being American, I had a hard time enforcing this rule; it is a definite gap in their upbringing. On the other hand, I had to teach them that saying, "*Bonjour, m'sieurs, dames*" (the abbreviation of "*Bonjour, messieurs; bonjour, mesdames*") is the height of vulgarity.

The *bise*, that light little kiss that just brushes the cheek, is great fun to try to figure out. An American guest of a friend of mine watched the pantomime of *bises* I gave my friend and her husband and her husband gave me and my husband and the children (about thirty-six *bises* in all) and exclaimed a bit huffily, "It doesn't mean anything"! Actually, it does mean something. The *bise* means you like the person more than if you just shook hands with him.

Of course, the American man had seen only *one* exchange of *bises;* he would be horrified to see the number of times a French family kisses in one day. In my French family, there is the bise before you go to bed and the bise when you get up in the morning. I avoid this morning one by saying that my teeth aren't brushed yet and by looking generally horrible enough to repel anyone who might want to approach.

One of the worst faux pas you can make in France is to drop in unexpectedly on a friend, even a good one. The French don't like to have unexpected visitors. In fact, they don't like much of anything unexpected. Never forget, as one American sagely pointed out, that unlike the United States, France is a one-time zone country, in which everyone is doing everything at just about the same time—hence a certain predictability in eating times, being home times, and bedtimes. Once I dropped in on a friend who was entertaining her parents. She kept me standing at the door, and it was obvious that she didn't want to introduce me to them. I could never figure out whether it was shame—of them? of me?—or whether you don't mix friends and family. But I tend to think it was the dropping in that precipitated what I felt was odd behavior.

Rituals, codes. These codified manners actually help to make life simpler—if you know the rules. As in a graceful minuet, each dancer knows the steps expected. Miss a step and the rhythm is broken. So it is with the decorum of French social life.

Curiously enough, there is no French Emily Post, Amy Vanderbilt, Miss Manners, or their equivalent, no one authority to consult to find out what to do and how to act. Perhaps because everyone old enough to read already knows how to behave? In any case, not to worry if you don't get all this down pat the first time around. I certainly didn't.

Just tell yourself that you could never, but never, attain the level of rudeness of a Parisian behind the wheel of his car. Nor, on the other hand, could you aspire to the heights of subtlety that constitute real French politesse. Should you put your foot in your mouth, or your giant lettuce leaf anywhere else, no one in France will embarrass you by howling with laughter. That most certainly is not done. At least not until you've left the room.

At the Table

Things to Do:

- Put your hands on, not under, the table.
- Decapitate your asparagus with knife and fork and eat only the tips.
- Cut Gruyère lengthwise, Roquefort so that the next person doesn't get all the white, and round cheeses in wedges.
- Take just what you'll eat and don't leave substantial amounts on the plate—*very* insulting.
- Converse lightly.

Things Not to Do:

- Don't eat with your hands (this includes pizza, fried chicken, barbecued spareribs, and even fruit).
- Don't cut your salad leaves with a knife and fork (a custom dating back to when the acidity of vinegar would rust the blade of the knife).

- Don't ask for toothpicks.
- Don't ask where the WC is—just go find it.
- Don't call the waiter "garçon." Instead, say, "S'il vous plaît?"
- Don't sop up the sauce with bread even if the bread is on a fork.
- Don't get soused—the French drink moderately.
- Don't yawn, especially with your mouth uncovered.
- Don't ask for coffee and dessert at the same time—they are separate courses.
- Don't get into a deep conversation on stocks and bonds—boring! Opt instead for a learned conversation on the world economic situation.

Interview with Philippe

HARRIET: *Why do you, a Frenchman, think that the French have a worldwide reputation for being quarrelsome and cantankerous?*

PHILIPPE: *Because we hate one another. But other than that, the language makes it sound like we're bawling one another out even when we aren't.*

We're just having fun. When we say something like "tête de veau" [head of a calf], it's just friendly.

HARRIET: *Why are the French so particularly rude and undisciplined in their cars?*

PHILIPPE: *We Frenchmen have a very Latin disrespect of the law. People who obey laws are considered stupid, so this makes France a very dangerous country. Also, a lot of Frenchmen put their virility in their cars.*

HARRIET: *Why is it that when a Frenchman asks you a question, he or she doesn't listen to a long, serious answer—or even pretend to?*

PHILIPPE: *Because the French don't like to have all the details (être besogneux). They like big ideas and the general picture.*

HARRIET: *You can say that again. . . . But back to rudeness. Why are the French nice to people they know and rude to everyone else?*

PHILIPPE: *That's a real difference. The people you don't know can die in front of you and no one cares. They are enemies, or potential enemies at least.*

HARRIET: *Is that why French people don't go overboard about welcoming newcomers/visitors/tourists?*

PHILIPPE: *Of course. As I said, the person you don't know may be an enemy. How many times have you been invaded? I myself have been invaded twice, first by the Germans, then by Euro Disneyland. You can never be too careful.*

School Daze

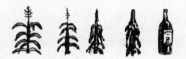

Why leave a discussion of the French educational system
to the end of these little reflections on French society?
Very frankly, a child's education is always a subject of
passion, and when you are putting your child in a foreign school
system, the subject becomes explosive. It may have taken me
a long time to get used to certain cultural differences,
but the one in which I have been the most personally involved,
for my children's sake, was that of education. The differences
between my education in the United States and my children's
education in French public schools were, very simply,
like night and day. It took a lot of getting used to.
And now that they are nearing the end of their
education . . . well, read on.

I decided that since their father was French and we were living in France, it would only be logical to send my two sons to French schools.

I didn't know it then, but I was in for a big change. First of all, although I speak fluent French, I realized that I would be of little or no help to my children when it came to the finer points of French grammar. I also realized that in a country where parents spend endless hours helping their kids with homework, I was an exception, feeling that it was more important for them to understand through their own mistakes. Helping with homework is so widespread that many French teachers will not accept typed papers because they fear that the work will be that of the parents, not the students. My inability to help my children turned out to be fortunate. They did the work themselves.

Second, I learned that in France, school is taken very seriously from day one. Students spend a lot of time studying and school is for learning, not for extracurricular activities.

The importance of school cannot be overestimated. Franco-American marriage counselor Jill Bourdais points out that in France "the cultural assumption is that children are supposed to spend all their time studying. In the States, parents want children to be well rounded. In France, kids have to do well in school or it's death. Schoolwork is a problem anywhere, but worse here for a Franco-American couple because of the cultural assumption toward this work and its importance."

Of all the things I learned, the most important one is the following valuable truism: *American mothers with children in French schools are much more traumatized by the whole experience than their kids are.* I italicize because this axiom turned out, I am convinced, to be the key to my own children's success in this system. My expectations of French schools were typically American. My children would learn, of course, but not just from books. Sports and music, debate and drama—all would play an important part. Teachers would never overtly criticize them or make them feel bad. And if something unpleasant happened, well, I would hightail it to the school and have a friendly little conversation with the teacher.

It just doesn't work that way in French schools. Teachers criticize students! Bad grades are given! School is work with a capital *W!* As an American mother of kids in French schools, I absolutely could not comprehend what was going on at school and decided to get my husband on the case—after all, he had gone through the system. Shouldn't he be the one to deal with it?

This decision turned out to be a miraculous stroke of good judgment. Suddenly, problems that had seemed insurmountable were cut down to size. As only a Frenchman with a command of the language and its nuances could, he would size up a situation, decide when it was worthwhile to intervene, and then do so with such aplomb, such perfect word choice, such lack of emotionalism, and such *sang-froid* that I was literally bowled over. "Leave the French educational system to those who have been through it!" I tell my friends. You won't believe what will happen.

A case in point: One day, a gym teacher accused my younger son of being sneaky, underhanded. We were very upset—first because of the public nature of the accusation and, second, because he had struggled with minor physical-coordination problems and we were afraid he would get down on gym and lose his self-confidence. I sent my husband to the school. Suddenly, there were no more complaints and gym seemed to be going all right. "What did you say to her?" I inquired. "I just told her that David hadn't spent five years of his life attending coordination-training sessions so that some gym teacher would mess it all up," he related calmly. But it wasn't just what he had said; it was the way he'd said it, *tout en finesse*. She got the message.

But even with a French husband to pave the way, there were many things I didn't know. I didn't know, for example, that if you even *think* you're going to have a baby, you sign him up for nursery school. I didn't know that little French kids routinely trot off to school at *age two*. So I was late, very late, and my first child didn't get into nursery school until the ripe old age of three.

Not having done what I was supposed to do, I had a

hard time. But politics finally prevailed in the form of a letter to the mayor of the sixteenth arrondissement, where I lived. "Dear sir," I penned, "I find it hard to believe that my son, Benjamin, who is now *two and a half*, has been deprived of six months of education. Surely something can be done for this poor child." Presto! By some miracle, a place was found in a school in our neighborhood. French politicians, like American ones, hate to disappoint their constituents.

Actually, this is a great system, especially for mothers who work. It's hard to see your little two-year-old wail as you leave him behind, but it gives mothers some valuable time from 9:00 A.M. to 4:00 P.M. In addition, the school organizes child care on the school premises from 4:00 P.M. to 6:00 P.M. so mothers who work in offices actually have an entire day to work and not have to pay a baby-sitter.

French nursery schools are probably the greatest invention of this system, not only for that reason but because the children themselves are generally pretty happy to get out of the house and be in a group of kids their own age.

The first time you leave your child is the hardest. Benjamin's school wasn't quite close enough to home for me to get him at noon, so it was decided that he would stay from 9:00 A.M. to 4:00 P.M. On the fateful first day, I led my blond, blue-eyed wee one to the school in fear and trepidation. Huge iron gates clanged shut and scores of tots cried their hearts out as they fastened their little bodies to the gates. Each and every one of those little tykes wanted his or her *maman*! Filled with guilt, I carried the image of my son's huge tear-filled eyes with me all day long. How could you abandon your child to school at that age?

I returned at the end of that long day, vowing to take him home with me until he was, say, five, a "normal" age for children to go to school. His teacher, a pretty, lively red-haired young woman, told me not to worry. After the initial shock of leaving his mother, Benjamin, it turned out, had a great time riding a tricycle and sleeping.

With one year of school under his belt, Benjamin, at the ripe old age of three years and eight months, was ready to start his second year of nursery school. This was the beginning of No More Messing Around. The first day, he wandered behind the school to play in the sandpile with a little comrade. The teacher didn't discover his absence until two hours later. Benjamin was so traumatized that he cried for two straight hours once he got home that night. I thought he would never go back to school again.

But he did. Meanwhile, the teacher who had lost him called me in and said, "Madame, your child is having drawing difficulties," which was a rather polite way of saying that his drawings were just plain weird. It turned out that they were entirely BLACK (probably his vision of school after having been lost the first day).

The next year at the venerable age of four and eight months, Benjamin got a conventional teacher of the old-school variety. Predictably, she had gray hair worn in a chignon. She scared *me*. Our contacts were limited to my timid questions about Benjamin's progress and her monosyllabic responses. But this was the year Benjamin learned to write, forming endless rows of *o*'s, *l*'s and *la*'s and *li*'s, sitting straight at his desk and not moving, the way little French children are taught to do. (Have you ever noticed how straight the French hold themselves, as opposed to the slouchy postures we Americans tend to adopt? This comes from years and years of teachers telling the students to sit up straight every time they get into a contorted position.)

By the time he entered primary school, he was thoroughly prepared to write, and write neatly—no light matter in a country where children are still expected, in many places, to write with fountain pens. Yes, fountain pens. As an American mother, it seemed logical to me that if a child is just learning to write, he should write with a pencil with an eraser so he would be able to rub out his mistakes—or a ballpoint or anything except a fountain pen, which is bound to create a mess.

No way.

My younger son, as I mentioned, had some coordination difficulties, which meant that writing with a fountain pen was extremely difficult and frustrating for him and all the pages of his notebooks were totally botched up. When I suggested that we just skip the fountain pen and have him write with a pencil or a ballpoint, the teachers—both at the public school he attended and at his special classes for handwriting—looked at me as if I were certifiably insane. Even when some of his teachers were sympathetic to his problem, they never relaxed their own standards of neatness. They hoped, obviously, to bring him "up" to these standards just as they would bring "up" a student who is poor in geography. In the end, they did.

The fountain pen story points out both the good and the bad side of French education. The good side is that the school nurse, during the regular yearly checkup, noticed that David was not physically coordinated and told both the teacher and us about it. The second time she tested him, she recommended we send him to special classes for handwriting problems. We did, two sessions a week for three years, and never spent a cent on it.

The downside was that, with the exception of two wonderful teachers, the other four he had in elementary school were, shall we say, not overly sympathetic to his problem.

But this may have its own logic in a system that is very strict. I mentioned my amazement about the whole issue of the fountain pen to his fifth-grade teacher, whom I liked and respected very much. I thought that, because she was so good with children, she might agree with me that the battle was really inane in the end. After all, she was one of the two teachers who told David he was great and who gave him the self-confidence he needed to write neatly.

Her reaction was not what I expected. She agreed that it is hard for children to write with a fountain pen at first. "But," she said, "we must teach them to confront difficulty; they need personal discipline. It isn't because a fountain pen is difficult that we should do away with the pen."

And that, for me, is the French system in a nutshell. Difficulties are there to be surmounted, not to be made easier. Concomitantly, this means, for the moment at least, that French students can't wiggle their way out of physics, chemistry, math, and all those "hard" subjects that students in the United States can manage to avoid for the rest of their lives after taking the bare minimum. Having been one of those students who cleverly managed to get out of anything too difficult and, notably, anything scientific, I tip my hat to a system where high school graduates have all been made to take the same basic fare—math, physics, chemistry, history, French, foreign languages, biology—for four years.

Many French parents are worried that the educational system is going down the drain; many yank their kids out of public schools and put them in private ones. We always preferred to keep our children in public schools and were fortunate enough to live in neighborhoods where they were good. If there's one conclusion I arrived at after putting my kids through French public schools, it's that no perfect system exists.

I found that compared to U.S. high schools, standards in French lycées are pretty high. When my son David was in the ninth grade, his summer reading list of books included works by Alexandre Dumas, Anatole France, George Orwell, and Ray Bradbury, as well as a modern French version of *Tristan and Isolde* by French medievalist René Louis. In eleventh grade, my son Benjamin (who progressed from weird black drawings to being a mathematics buff) read books by Honoré de Balzac, Victor Hugo, Edgar Poe, and Émile Zola, among others. For me, the way French education sticks to the classics is an advantage (excuse me, all you PC types out there).

Sometimes there is a lack of communication between a teacher and the parents. But generally you can get everything worked out via a little notebook the children are given at the beginning of the year. In it, the teacher can write things such as "David was very noisy in class today. This must cease." In this way, parents are aware of what is going on in the class. This is handy, because French schools are definitely not open houses. The teachers' job is to teach, the administrators' to administrate, and the parents' to keep their distance unless specifically invited to the school.

Sometimes we American mothers don't understand certain punishments that seem to be par for the course.

My friend Jan was furious because her daughter, age nine, had been made to stand up for forty-five minutes in the corridor as a punishment. I related the story to my son David, then age fourteen. "So what's the problem?" he asked philosophically. "That used to happen to me all the time." That was the first wind I had ever had of that!

It's true that, by American standards, French teachers can be hard on students. They don't mince their words. They're not afraid of the school board! A teacher in a French school will not hesitate to tell a kid that he is a lousy, terrible student with no future, and what is he doing in her class, anyway? My niece, while taking her oral exams at the Sorbonne, was told by a professor that she hoped that her other grades were good, because, she said, "with the grade I'm giving you, you'll need all the help that you can get."

In a French school, work has to be really special to get an *A*. French teachers mark from zero to twenty, with twenty being an almost inaccessibly high mark. When last in Iowa, a math teacher in my former high school told me that if he dared give a *C-* or, heaven help him, anything lower, the parents would bring the matter up with the school board, and he would get fired. An elementary school teacher in Arizona told me she quit her job because she had been giving *C*'s to the children in her class who weren't doing well, and since many of them were Hispanic, she was accused of discrimination.

In France, this political correctness—or fear for your job if you don't hand out good grades—is nonexistent. In fact, at two different schools where I taught, I was asked to redo my grades and downgrade them. The director called me in and apologized: "I know that in America you tend to give high grades, but, you see, here the curve is much lower." I didn't protest. It's their system. A colleague told me that the director of a very prestigious school he taught in personally administered a dressing-down to the faculty for the high marks they were giving their remarkably gifted students. "We can't have any more of this," he yelled. A faculty member responded ironically, "Why don't we just give them all *C*'s and *D*'s in that case?" But that's the system. One must aim for perfection.

Yet there are few complaints. French students are used to seeing an *A* or *A+* as an almost unattainable goal, and when they do finally get a high mark, they know it means something.

Of course you need high standards in a country where only a chosen few will make it to the very top—the *grandes écoles*. Many French parents, like many American parents, have big ambitions for their kids from the time they set foot in kindergarten. (I realize this is true on the East Coast of the United States; we were spared this pressure in Iowa.) I'll never forget Claudie, my son's kindergarten teacher, telling me, "You're so different from the other parents." I asked, "Why?" She said, "Because you just want your son to have a good time and you aren't pushing him." I replied, "Why would I push the kid? He's only five, after all." And she responded, "Oh, there are parents who want Pierre to go to *Polytechnique* and are already putting on the pressure."

"What's *Polytechnique*?" I asked. I don't remember her answer, but I do remember that it took me years to understand the French system of *grandes écoles*, of which *Polytechnique* is one of the most, if not the most, prestigious. Now that my twenty-year-old is in one of these schools, I at long last understand the *grandes écoles* system but find myself in serious trouble when trying to explain it to my American family. It's so typically French!

In a nutshell, the *grandes écoles* were created by Napoléon to form a corps of elites. These schools are different from the university because any student with his baccalaureate degree from high school can go to the university. This means that universities are overcrowded and that many students give up and drop out. In contrast, students entering the *grandes écoles* have gone through a rigorous selection process, notably two years of preparatory school after the baccalaureate. During these two years, they prepare to take the stiff qualifying exams that will determine if they get in a *grande école* and which school they qualify for. Classes in the *grandes écoles* are smaller, and once you get in, it is highly unusual to flunk out.

One day, after my sister had insisted on Benjamin's coming to the United States for a year, I could see that she didn't understand that he *couldn't,* because if you are on this track in France, you can't get off it, and so I tried to explain all of this to my family.

"Yes, you see, Benjamin graduated from high school but there was no graduation ceremony, no gowns, no music, no prom, no diploma handed out. His high school diploma, in fact, was mailed to him several months later. And since his grades in math during school and on the baccalaureate exam [and then I had to explain that this is a national exam that all French kids take prior to leaving high school] were excellent, he qualified for a prep school, so in two years he can take exams to try to get into what the French call a *grande école.*"

At about this point, my family members started getting mystified. If he's so good, why didn't he just go on to the university? No, I explained, in France, it's the reverse of what happens in the United States: If you're really good, you *don't* go to the university. You go to a special prep school where there's a steady diet of math and science for the kids who are excellent in scientific studies, or literature for kids who excel in the arts, and after a two-year grind, the ones who are left take competitive exams to enter the *grandes écoles.*

This explanation sparked a flicker of interest from my mom, who, as a former teacher, is very interested in education in general and my sons' education in particular.

"And where is this preparatory school he is attending?"

"It's in a high school, Mom," I said, and I suddenly realized this whole thing appeared too strange to be real. My son had graduated from high school and was now studying in a high school. . . . I could see by the look on her face that she was confused.

"In a high school?" she said.

"Yes, it's in a high school." I beamed. "But of course these are no longer high school students, so they have entirely separate classes. They are in classes from about nine A.M. to six P.M. five days a week and on Saturday morning, and they have a minimum of three hours of homework after school. Twice a week, they have what the French call '*colles*' [oral exams]. They are given a really difficult topic and have to discourse on it for an hour. When they're not in school, they are at home doing their homework. They have no time for outside activities."

I took a deep breath. "*But*, at the end of the two years, after they have suffered through this grind and are but pale fragile remnants of what they once were, they have been thoroughly trained to take these stiff exams. Depending on the score they get, they will be admitted to the best schools in the nation. For those who want to be teachers or researchers, this school would be the *École Normale Supérieure* followed by *Polytechnique* for engineering. And once they get into these schools, they can relax and cool it and kind of do what they want."

"Oh, I didn't know Benjamin wanted to be an engineer!"

"He doesn't, Mom. But in France, if you're smart and good in math, and even if you don't want to be an engineer, you have to follow this track, because if not, you would go off to the university with everyone else, and classes at the university are overflowing. No one pays any attention to you there, and when you get out, your diploma is worth almost nothing."

"My goodness! But what does Benjamin want to do?"

"He doesn't really know. He thinks he wants to be a teacher. But all this is immaterial at this point. What he has to do is go through the preparatory classes, pass his exams, and make it into a *grande école*. Then he will be able to choose."

"He will make it of course, but, well, what if he didn't?"

"Then he would have to go to the university with everyone else."

My mother by now was totally lost, and I realized that she must have thought that her grandson had probably flunked out of high school and was doing some kind of remedial course somewhere.

Of course, it's just the opposite. Having taught in the

grandes écoles, I can affirm that the kids who are there are the crème de la crème in terms of standing up under pressure, working like dogs, and assimilating an enormous amount of information.

Los Angeles Times correspondent Stanley Meisler, who lived in France for five years, puts it better than I do: "The best graduates of the French educational system have a precision of mind, command of language and store of memory that would make the heart of most American educators ache with envy. It is doubtful that any school system in the world teaches more logic and grammar or offers more courses."

However, he adds—and this is indeed the catch—". . . a sobering price is paid. Precision in thought and beauty of language are the products of an elite French school system that is repressive, frightening and stifling to many pupils who cannot keep up. There is no tolerance or time for spontaneity or weakness."

My younger son decided to opt for the university route, so now I will be able to compare the *grande école* system and the university system from personal experience and not just hearsay. What I can see for the moment is that while my elder son's struggle was limited to the two grueling years of *prépa* before he entered his *grande école,* the challenge for my younger will be to find his place within a system in which thousands of students are enrolled and no one is going to pay any particular attention to them. In the university system, the route the vast majority of French students take, students have little to no contact with professors, don't live on a campus, and have to sink or swim in a system in which they are just a number. In spite of this, I'm optimistic and believe that each will receive an excellent education. Whether a *grande école* or a university, education in France is excellent. It just isn't all that easy, but as you will see in the interview with Philippe, making things easy for students apparently isn't a value in the French educational system.

Before I started teaching in France, I had no idea that when you get in front of a class, you are supposed to wipe that smile off your face and look serious. I was in for a big surprise.

If you go into a classroom in France, you will probably see that the teacher's desk is on a raised platform. In most cases, the teacher is not conceived of as an equal and is always addressed with the polite *vous*.

French students think of a teacher as someone who should have a certain dignity and be thought of as a bit above them. They look at you like you're a nutcase if you indulge in "unprofessorial" behavior. I know. In the courses I gave at the *Institut d'Études Politiques* (the French equivalent of the London School of Economics), I would very naturally gesticulate, grimace, and smile to make a point. As I did so, I could see the students in front of me knitting their brows and laughing nervously. They were clearly puzzled.

By the same token, I have been stymied over the years by students (generally women, for some odd reason) whose facial expressions indicate either extreme boredom or extreme disapproval (with me? with the class?). Each time, it turned out that there was no particular problem—it was just their normal nonsmiling expression. Apparently, smile=idiot.

In any case, French students just don't take a smiling teacher seriously. An American teacher of English in the *grandes écoles* system told me that she had failed a student, first of all because he had not even attended the number of classes required to get a minimum passing grade and, second, because when he did make it to class, he made no effort at all to participate. When he discovered that she had actually failed him, he was furious—not just because of the grade but because he didn't understand how badly he had been doing.

My friend explained the situation to him: "I told you many times that you would have to do better, but I didn't yell at you because I didn't want you to get a mental block about English." He shook his head wonderingly. "No teacher has ever told me something like that," he said, adding, "I thought that because you weren't yelling at me, that I was okay, that the class was very relaxed, and that you would pass me."

"No," she told him, "I was telling you in as many ways as I could without humiliating you."

His reply was, "But you were smiling when you said it." The student, by the way, was twenty-three, old enough to read the instructions for failing grades but convinced that if the teacher was smiling, she wouldn't fail him and they would work something out. Of course, this wasn't true, but he was fooled by her relaxed manner, which did not correspond in any way, shape, or form to the reserved, dignified, and distant authority figure French students are used to.

The biggest compliment I ever got in my life was from a French student who wrote me, "Your teaching seems profoundly spontaneous, free of any formal constraints and useless rules; it is 'free.'" This obviously was a big change for him, and I'm not at all convinced that the school administration would consider this attribute of spontaneity a plus.

The twenty-three-year-old probably would have understood a more frank reaction—French teachers can be *very* forthright. I thought at one point that perhaps my kids would like to go to an American school, where teachers tend to be gentler. They both refused categorically. Commented David at the time, "I prefer brusque teachers. I don't want them to encourage me. I prefer them to tell me that my work is insufficient or bad rather than for them to say, 'It is not as good today.'"

What he doesn't like, however, is that as soon as the

teacher hands back homework, all the kids jump around to find out what grade the others got. Encouraging competition is the whole point, of course, as the system is based on survival of the fittest. "Since I have been in fourth grade, we've been told about the bac and the *grandes écoles*. They tell us to be good students, because if not, we won't get our bac," said David, who by ninth grade was becoming wise to the ways of the world.

I'll never forget my elder son's French bac (the baccalaureate exam has been divided so that when kids are juniors, they take only the French exam; the next year, they take exams in all the other subjects). I don't know why Benjamin was so nervous. I mean, all he had to do was study Baudelaire, Rimbaud, and Marivaux and be able to discourse knowledgeably on such themes as "the birth of love in French literature" at the ripe old age of sixteen—first in an oral exam, alone with one professor for forty minutes (twenty minutes to prepare and twenty for his presentation), then in a written exam that lasts four hours.

Benjamin decided that the only thing he disliked more than French was philosophy, a subject of the following year's exam. When it came time for the four-hour test, he got a choice of several subjects, including "Is the truth always credible? and "Isn't work just a way for man to satisfy his needs?"

My son made the mistake (in my opinion) of choosing the third subject, an excerpt from a text of Sartre's that starts like this: "The meaning of the past is tightly dependent on my present project. This does not mean that I can change at whim the sense of my past actions, but, on the contrary, that the fundamental project that I am following determines absolutely the meaning—for myself and for others—of the past that I must be." Excuse the rough translation—are you still with me?

The text continues like this for another nine lines and concludes, "Who can judge the learning value of a trip, the sincerity of a pledge of love, the purity of a past intention, etc.? It is I, it is I, according to the end by which I make them explainable." After reading the passage, the students were asked to discourse on the "philosophical interest of this text" through an "orderly study" of it.

Benjamin refused to see the philosophical interest of any of this. As an American mother, I had a hard time seeing how any seventeen-year-old would have the maturity to comprehend, let alone discuss, any of these subjects. My French husband said that both Benjamin and I were *inculte* (lacking culture). Another cultural breach . . .

France, in fact, is the only country in the world to require philosophy as a subject for high school students. This is why the French generally reason from the general to the particular and don't think in terms of "Here's a problem; I must find a solution." What's important is to think about problems and be able to ask questions.

In spite of his feeling about philosophy, Benjamin is an excellent student who has interiorized the system to the point where, when I asked him if he would like to continue tennis lessons during his two years of preparation for the entrance exams to the *grandes écoles,* he answered thanks but no thanks, since he would have to spend all his time studying. Of course he's a case; he's the kind of serious, mature kid who would have surprised everyone if he hadn't gone on to a *grande école.*

It goes without saying that French children of our social class, educational level, and aspirations (writing this, it occurred to me that perhaps it's just our children) do not clean house. You do not even think of asking a kid to do something like ironing or vacuuming, not to mention doing the dishes or even taking out the garbage on a regular basis. My kids will clear the table, empty wastebaskets, and keep their rooms clean because they have to, but that's about it.

One reason that parents like me accept this is that children on this educational track are supposed to be devoted to their schoolwork to the exclusion of everything else. Everything else, my sons assure me, includes cleaning. Since they have so much schoolwork and are in school so long every day, how could any parent expect them to come home and pitch in on anything?

The amount of homework French kids do astounds

most Americans, who are used to being pretty cool about school, especially high school and, even more so, grade school. "One thing that shocked me," a twenty-five-year-old American au pair working for a French family with three children told me, "was to see the six-year-old boy with a half hour of homework to do after being in school from eight-forty-five A.M. to four-thirty P.M. The two eleven-year-olds in the family had forty-five minutes of work every night." When my son Benjamin was in preparatory school, he spent a full day at school, many days returning at 7:00 P.M. After dinner, he studied until midnight—and he was by far the least hardworking of his classmates!

It's true that the French system is geared to those who succeed, that there's a good deal of work, and that not everyone is suited to this rigorous system. Kids are expected to meet high standards and the system can be a bit inflexible at times. And not all French teachers would win the world championship for creativity or consideration of students' feelings.

But there are some important advantages. Other than books, school supplies, and school lunches, the cost of my sons' education—both through high school and beyond, all through university or the *grandes écoles*—was zero. Considering the level of their studies and the high standards students are expected to meet, what the French call *rapport qualité/prix* (cost-effectiveness) couldn't be better.

It's true that in this discussion on education, I have focused on the elite and the *grandes écoles* (I wonder why—after all, the entire French system is focused on the elite) and didn't get into the multiple problems of education in suburbs, where the kids raise Cain and the teachers wonder whether they are there to teach or be social workers. That's a whole other story, and since I'm writing from my personal experience, I opted to stick to what I have personally experienced. It's been a long haul and wasn't always easy, but in the end I'm glad I stuck it out—and anyway, what's done is done! I really truly think that I suffered more from the French educational system and my feelings about it than my children ever did. They're fine, thank you!

And just think—while the kids are studying, they're off the streets, not riding around in cars or taking drugs. And since school is based on work and not extracurricular activities, there is an astonishing lack of peer pressure. True, my kids didn't star on the basketball team, because there wasn't one. Ditto for band. They will, though, have received a complete education in terms of knowledge. And, hey, they have the rest of their lives to develop their personalities. That, definitely, is not the job of the French public school.

Interview with Philippe

HARRIET: *What do you think is the major difference between American and French education?*

PHILIPPE: *You don't educate children by teaching them basketball. In France, there's no basketball university or Ph.D. in baseball.*

HARRIET: *Don't you think you're a bit snobbish?*

PHILIPPE: *You think that in school you should have fun; I think that in school you should study. We'll never agree on that point.*

HARRIET: *What about the* grandes écoles? *This system is totally incomprehensible to anyone outside France.*

PHILIPPE: *The system of* grandes écoles *is just a special form of university. But since there's no football field, it's not considered a university—by you. I am very upset that you never understood—or say you didn't—the system of* grandes écoles, *in spite of the fact that I went to one. This is very insulting.*

HARRIET: *What about these mean teachers who don't care a fig for the feelings of their students?*

PHILIPPE: *What about the mean boss, the mean Serbs, the mean serial killers? French education forms children for what they are going to see later on in life. The American system of education forms children who will be surprised by what they see later on. French teachers aren't clowns. They aren't paid to entertain children. They're not baby-sitters. They're professors.*

HARRIET: *You say that French education is great because it's free. What are you thinking about in particular?*

PHILIPPE: *We never saved money to send our children to university. Thank God, because with you, it would have been hard, if not impossible. [Author's note: Ha-ha. Very funny.] This is a fundamental point. We have gone to restaurants for the past twenty years and never once thought, Is this meal depriving our children of a university education?*

Why I'll Never Be French
(But I Really Am!)

As we near the end of *French Toast,* we arrive at the
most important part: why I say I'll never be French.

When people learn that I have lived in France a little
over two decades, the inevitable comment is, "Then you
must have become French." My spontaneous answer to
that comment is, "No." But upon deeper reflection, I
have to say that while in many circumstances the cultural gap is, if anything, only greater, in others I feel that
I have indeed become "almost" French.

I have come to accept and love customs that seemed
strange to me at first. For example, I was a bit surprised
by country weekends that revolved entirely around food,
but it didn't take long at all to slip right into, and

become a champion of, the tradition of the long, lei-surely meal hour. I thought the *baisemain* was a tad strange, but I have to confess that I rather like it now or, shall we say, at least I don't pull my hand away! I ap-preciate the lack of pressure to join groups. At one point, we lived in a small suburb of Nantes where the neighbors, mostly Catholic, were building floats for a religious parade. We're not Catholic, but we were made to feel welcome to join in if we wished, or just stand by if we didn't. Not being a joiner, I am grateful for this freedom.

Freedom from worry about medical bills is another major reason I appreciate living in France. Another plus is that doctors still pay house calls. Never once did I have to pry a feverish child from his sickbed to "go see the doctor." The doctor came to us! For me, this is the mark of an eminently civilized country.

French vacations are pretty civilized as well. I love, and am slowly getting used to, planning for a minimum of five weeks vacation a year and sometimes as many as eight. I am still not French, though, in the sense that I haven't quite got it down to barely finishing one vaca-tion and then immediately planning the next. But I am rapidly getting there. For example, in June I start pan-icking about what my sons will be doing for their Christmas vacation.

I like the fact that the word *no* does not mean what it does in Anglo-Saxon or Germanic countries. *No* invariably means that the person in question does not want to bother. However, if you stand there long enough and wait him or her out, you generally get what you want.

This freedom to do what you want, more or less, has its good and bad sides. Like most foreigners, I take the good for myself and look at the bad as a necessary evil I have to live with. Smoking, for example. The good side is that the French government has decided to do something about smoke in public places, and the bad side is that many a smoker is choosing to ignore the NO SMOKING signs and sanctions. In spite of the new no-smoking rules, it will be a long time, if ever, before you can be sure of going into a restaurant and not having some dude breathe smoke into your lungs as you try to enjoy your *boeuf bourguignon.*

Don't bring up the sensitive subject of smoking unless you are prepared to argue about it at length. This happened to a friend of mine who had finally gone out for an evening alone with her husband. At the restaurant they were sitting in, she remarked to the man next to her that she would appreciate it if he wouldn't smoke his cigar in her face. That touched off a debate with the offender—on Americans, puritanism, smoking in general, politeness—that lasted right through the meal, while he continued to smoke and my friend seethed.

"But," says another American who has also been here twenty years, "at least they aren't puritanical about it. In the United States, they treat you like a leper." This confirms a particularly attractive Latin characteristic of the French, little or no moralizing. In this vein, most French people think Jim and Tammy Bakker and their public confessions of sin on TV are just plain grotesque and that Richard Nixon's downfall was a downright shame. After all, it's a well-known fact that all politicians lie, isn't it? And as far as fads are concerned, whether it is the no-smoking fad, jogging, or being politically correct, the French just won't go for it. They're too busy fighting among themselves to agree on anything.

As for fighting, I am far too Anglo-Saxon to actually enjoy a dispute, and I could certainly go without a fight a day to keep me in shape. On the other hand, I have grown to appreciate the fact that you can have it out with people without resorting to violence. As my French husband pointed out, verbal fighting is merely jousting, not to be taken too seriously. "It's no fun to pick fights with Americans," he says, and adds, with his characteristic Gallic sense of hyperbole, "There's no intermediate level of aggression. It's either a big smile and be nice or pick up a gun."

Indeed, it does seem like everyone is always fighting over something (the language lends itself to this). My American family has been convinced that everything was going up in smoke, when in fact all my husband and I were discussing was what wine to have with dinner.

When in France, you have to know how to express your emotions. In other words, you have to know how to spend time dealing with others on a confrontational basis. This can be over simple things such as getting cheated on change or having it out with a taxi driver who is free but who is just not in the mood to take you to where you want to go.

If you are a self-respecting Frenchman, you get mad. As a phlegmatic Anglo-Saxon, even after twenty years here, I fume inwardly but just can't manage to external-ize it the way the French do so admirably. *"Tête de veau,"* my husband yells at another driver as we slalom through a traffic jam. Cowering in the seat beside him, I'm sure I have just seen my final moments. *Mais non.* The other driver shouts something even worse.

One typical day, I was driving down a one-way street and what did I see in front of me but a small white Peu-geot whose driver had left the car, with lights flashing, in the middle of the street. When the owner of the Peu-geot finally showed up ten minutes later, instead of apologizing for the inconvenience, he deigned to look me in the eye and say, "What's the matter? Are you in a hurry?" I'll *never* get used to this cavalier way of treat-ing other human beings, no matter how long I live in this country.

The most extraordinary discovery I made, after twenty years of living here, is that being nice is not high on the list of values. On the contrary, if you are constantly nice, you are seen as one big *poire* (sucker). Hence, since being nice is not something people set out to do, getting treated nicely is a totally unpredictable occurrence. As one observer noted, "Americans are nice to people they don't know yet; the French are nice to the people they know." That explains why you often see dogs in butcher shops (underneath the sign that says NO DOGS ALLOWED) and in restaurants, and smokers all over the place, because no one feels any deep obligation not to bother people one does not know. Who cares?

"The Frenchman," wrote Henry Miller, "protects the vessel which contains the spirit." Perhaps only the French could have invented the expression for the way they deal with life: *ils se défendent*. They defend themselves against the unknown, against others. If you get a crowd of French people who don't know one another, the results can range from excruciating to hilarious. An American friend of mine, who didn't know any better, threw a big party, composed entirely of French neighbors who didn't know one another. By the end of the evening, no one had said a word. This basic suspicion of others, which governs social life, is very French, and so, if you live here long enough, you soon learn to be on your guard and defend yourself. Where else but in France could you hear someone remark sarcastically to a new acquaintance who is getting too familiar, "*On n'a pas gardé les cochons ensemble.*" ("We didn't keep the pigs together.") Or "*Est-ce-que je vous demande si votre grand-mère fait du vélo?*" ("Did I ask you if your grand-mother rides a bike?") Private life is really private life.

The French love to challenge authority. If it is there, it is to be contested. I used to be shocked that the only sign of national unity I could see in the French was their solidarity against authority. The general rule of thumb seems to be solidarity against the state—and, very frankly, when you see the way many French cops act (snotty, as if they'd love to throw you in jail if they could only think up a way), you've got to hand it to the French for warning one another against them. One day I was in the car with a French friend who had run a red light she hadn't seen. When the policeman drew up alongside the car, instead of getting small and humble, she started bawling him out. Having gotten out of the situation without a ticket, she turned to me and laughed: "You've always got to be on the offensive; otherwise, you're a goner," she said.

French cops can be lenient, depending on their mood and your powers of persuasion. It's up to you to try to get out of what you've gotten into, and from then on, it's a question of karma. One day in a fit of impatience, I peeled out of a traffic jam and crossed a white line, a very serious and costly traffic offense. My hope was that no one would see me, but as luck would have it, I drove right into a pack of police on hand for the express purpose of arresting idiots like me. I tried a new tactic (and, I am convinced that I succeeded also because I was well dressed and feeling rather charming that particular day): I looked straight at the officer with total abandon and said, "There's nothing I can say, Officer. I am totally in the wrong. I admit it." Then I hunkered down in what I considered an appropriately humble yet optimistic pose as he rounded my car (a technique the cops use to see what they can find, and they generally find something). He hadn't even gone halfway when he appeared at my window: "Go on," he said, smiling, "and don't ever do it again." I fairly sped away, hoping he wouldn't be contradicted by one of his fellow *flics*.

Although I said I would never be French, I applied for and was granted French nationality just a few months ago. Why? Because in the end, I'm here because I want to be. (Also, the U.S. government finally gave the green light allowing citizens to have double nationality, so you can believe I jumped on that one.) So, although I'll never BE French, I now am the proud possessor of a French passport and a French identity card. From now on, when I criticize or praise the French, one could say that I am criticizing or praising myself, as well.

In spite of all the things that I appreciate about the French and even the ways in which I myself feel almost French, there are still a number of things that daily prove to me that I will never, ever be French.

The French will never get me to abandon my perhaps naïve belief that the customer is always right. I'm always shocked when a haughty salesperson drives me out of a store. However, after twenty years of experience, I still don't know how to deal with this. My French friends do, though.

One day, one of them went to buy a pan for fish in a department store. After finally locating the department, he told the saleslady that he was interested in buying an aluminum fish cooker, not the stainless-steel kind she was showing him. "I don't talk to people who eat in aluminum," she proclaimed, and started to walk away. My reaction would probably have been to slink away in disgrace, muttering to myself. My French friend drew himself up and glacially ordered her to get her boss. Moral of the story: Always go straight to the top.

As far as teacher-pupil relationships are concerned, I'll never get used to the negative attitudes French teachers have toward their students. Having grown up in a nation where the goal is to encourage even the worst of students, it is hard for me to see students I consider as not bad at all being treated as if they were *nul* (zero).

In any case, French attitudes toward children in general are very different from American attitudes. Americans explain what they are trying to get across. The French, at least in my husband's traditional French family—and in many others I know, as well—don't waste so much time being diplomatic. "You do this because

I said so" is not seen as a terrorist threat. The lines are clearly drawn, and it is unusual to see parents engaging in negotiations with their kids.

One example comes to mind: A young American couple entered a Chinese restaurant in the Latin Quarter with their son. A normal two-year-old, the toddler proceeded to fiddle with the chopsticks (and almost rammed one into his ear), upset the water glass, and run around the restaurant. The parents began by reasoning with him, explaining that he had to be good.

My French husband watched the scene in wonder. For him, it was obvious that you don't take a two-year-old to a restaurant; that if you do, he is expected to behave in a civilized fashion; and, most important, you don't negotiate with a two-year-old. I remember that one of the only times I ever got upset with my mother-in-law was when my son was that age and she was definitely not amused by one of his antics, one which I found cute.

It's not that my husband or in-laws or the French in general hate kids, although if you stick around Paris long enough, you may begin to wonder about that. It's just that children in France have traditionally been seen as little adults and therefore there is a low tolerance for too much childish behavior. Lawrence Wylie, the Harvard professor who wrote a book about the town of Roussillon, where he lived for a year with his family, observed that the French were astonished when he had his kids stay home with a baby-sitter instead of taking them along for village get-togethers. In France, especially in small towns, children are included in family get-togethers once they know how to participate without monopolizing the conversation.

In fact, the concept of children as children and not as miniature adults is a relatively recent one in French history. That's why when a French kid comes up with a funny remark, no one makes too much of it. He's a kid all right, but on his way to becoming an adult. One fortunate result of this that I have often seen, in my own home and that of others, is that children brought up this way do not dominate conversations. In fact, on several occasions, non-French visitors have asked me if my kids are okay, because they didn't say much at the table. I assured them that they were indeed okay (I didn't add that they are really silly in private) but that their French father had trained them never to interrupt an adult conversation.

After a certain age, children are invited to the table with the adults, sit there until very late, even are allowed to taste wine, but never do they become the object of the conversation. They participate, but they don't dominate. They are included, but not to the exclusion of an adult conversation. The good part of this is that they learn to listen to adults and form their own ideas. The adults are happy to have them around and don't feel they are a nuisance or have to be excused.

The flip side of the coin is that French children, forced to be so well behaved around their parents or other grown-ups *("Bonjour, madame")*, are often quite noisy or ill-behaved when released from adult supervision. All that bossing has a perverse effect. The children are very well behaved in front of adults, and then, behind their backs, are perfectly horrible—rather like the proverbial preacher's kid.

I got another point of view on this from an American fellow who was working as an au pair. He told me he thought that "French children are obnoxious and very badly behaved by American standards. I think French parents are much more permissive in terms of what they let their children do." I laughed with delight at these observations, I must say, because for years I had been hearing that American children, mine and others, are horrible little savages. In addition, in France I had encountered very few permissive parents.

I would qualify our family as somewhere halfway between law and order and liberalism. My sons tell me that they have friends whose parents won't let them watch TV or listen to rock music. One of my elder son's friends came to our place for the first time and stopped dead in his tracks when he saw Benjamin's room, which was covered with posters of heavy-metal rock stars. "You mean your parents let you put those on the wall?" he asked my eighteen-year-old incredulously. "And they let you play Iron Maiden?" He couldn't believe it. And

I couldn't believe there are parents who don't let their kids listen to what they want, no matter how much they hate it, and boy, do I hate it! But many French parents, particularly those who have children in the *grandes écoles*, are determined not to have their attention diverted from their studies.

Most French children maintain family ties long after they are grown, either because they really do like their families or because a family comes in handy. Given their reserve, making friends is a difficult task so it is easier to call on the family than on friends. Whereas in the United States a mother might call up her next-door neighbor to take care of Johnny, in France the child is much more likely to go straight to his *mamie* (grandma). Sunday dinners are obligatory occasions, during which *mamie* cooks for everyone, and *maman* and *papa*, even if full-grown, assume the roles of children. Many French families spend their entire vacations together, either in their country home or in a place they rent together. When the family gathers, it is the mother who makes and enforces the rules, which everyone follows. The sons and daughters fall back into being the sons and daughters of their parents, rather than the mothers and fathers of their children!

Language, ironically enough, is another thing that separates me from the French, for in spite of fluency, I am plagued with an accent. And your accent follows you everywhere. For the past twenty years, every time I open my mouth and say more than two words, people ask, "Are you English or American?" In France, you can have an accent and of course be French—many naturalized Frenchmen have accents—but you know in your heart of hearts that until the day you speak French without an accent, you can never really be French.

The French have such a thing about their language that they will do perfectly abominable things, such as making overt fun of your accent. What I hate the most are the instant imitators. These are the people who hear you say two words and then imitate those two words with your accent—for example, *très bien.* "*Très bien*," they parrot with a perfect American accent in French. This may seem hilariously funny to them, but I am *not amused* to hear my own accent thrown back in my face.

One evening, I was at a dinner with an eminent French doctor who did this for the entire duration of the meal. By the end of it, I was out of my mind with rage and humiliation. On another occasion, I put up with a Frenchman's horribly accented English without saying a word—I was brought up to be polite—and when his wife joined us and we started speaking French, she started imitating my accent. On yet another occasion, a very good friend of my husband's looked at me and declared, "When you talk, it's like a caricature of an American speaking French." Thanks, buddy. My husband's friend, by the way, doesn't speak a word of English.

Being on the receiving end of that for the past twenty years has put me in a pretty aggressive state of mind, and I must admit that when I see it coming, I start yelling (in French), *"Don't even start doing that. I won't take it."* It doesn't make me the most popular person at the party, but at least it makes things clear.

Otherwise, you're in for comments such as "You must be kidding. You can't have arrived twenty years ago. And you still have that accent?" Oh well . . . It's not just me. It happens to all my friends who are burdened with that visible verbal stamp that says, I'm not French. As it happens, I do have American friends who, fortunately for them, speak beautifully unaccented French; this makes their lives much easier.

"People make fun of your accent because they *like* it," my husband explained to me. "Did you ever see anyone making fun of a German accent?" Oh, *great*, I thought. "Which means," I asked him, "that if you like something, you make fun of it?" Are these twisted values or what? But, here again, this may go back to the French educational system, where teachers make fun of students all the time. It probably feels good to be able to do it to somebody else.

Polite, cultivated Frenchmen (generally those who speak another language and know the difficulties entailed) say, "Oh, I really love an American accent," or, better still, lie: "You hardly have any accent at all." I *love* those people, and fortunately there are a lot of them.

My husband has a very slight accent in English. While in Jay's Drugstore in Shenandoah on a once-in-a-lifetime visit, he sat down and ordered a Coke. The waitress came up to him, bent over, and yelled in his ear, "Did you say a COKE? A LARGE OR A SMALL ONE?" She figured that talking louder would surely straighten him out. So it does happen the other way around, but for the moment, I'm the one with the greatest number of incidents to report on the accent front.

Of course, one might say I deserve it. As a child, we had only one person in town who had an accent. She called one day, and thinking it was a friend of my sister's imitating the woman, I yelled for my sister, making fun of the person on the phone. My mother and sister immediately let me know how disappointed they were in me for being so cruel. But not to worry. I am paying for that inconsiderate childhood act every day of my life.

My accent-afflicted friends and I are currently devising several solutions to this mockery. Being Americans, we first thought of guns. But being antiguns, we settled on a water pistol, which we would squirt at the surprised offender. A more peaceful solution: a sandwich board with the message YES I HAVE LIVED HERE FOR OVER TWENTY YEARS. I STILL HAVE AN ACCENT. SO WHAT ARE YOU GOING TO DO ABOUT IT? Yet another is immediate: Start speaking English to the offender. This causes instant embarrassment, as the majority of people who make fun of accents don't speak any English at all.

But, I admit, we still haven't stumbled upon the perfect solution, other than taping our mouths shut forever. There's an idea!

Do I sound hostile or obsessed about the accent subject? I talked to a German air hostess, who told me that she had lived in the States for more than twenty years and every time she opened her mouth, she got the "Where are you from?" bit, just as I do. It made me feel *so* much better. Anyway, I am hatching up a secret plan, which is to hire an accent professor who will teach me once and for all to get those *r*'s and *u*'s down pat. I'll let you know if it works. Until then, au revoir, with the accent included. My name, by the way, has *four r*'s in it. *Quelle horreur!*

Accents are a problem—unless you speak French with a French accent. But let's say that you do speak perfect French with a French accent. You've still got to get down the subtle art of the lingo, such as expressing a positive thought in the negative.

Another language difference is the highly developed art of understatement. When you drink a glass of the most wonderful Bordeaux you have ever had in your life, you don't raise the glass and exclaim, *"Merveilleux!"* You sniff it, sip it, and then say, with a considered frown,

"*Ca se laisse boire.*" ("It's palatable.") The French speak in negatives, rather than positives, so rather than saying the weather is nice, they say it is *pas mauvais* (not bad). If a French person sees a newborn baby, he will say, "*Il n'est pas vieux, hein?*" ("He's not old, huh?")

If you're really gifted, you learn to combine understatement with the negative form. For example, the day my son got 19.5 out of 20 on a math test, his teacher wrote, "*Pas mal.*" ("Not bad.") You have to be French to understand and appreciate this "second-degree" humor. That is to say that in any case, the teacher might have put "Not bad," but since the grade was so good, it was funnier and more creative to put "Not bad" than just "Great." Get it?

But on to something more subtle still. Even if you have the language down pat, as many people do, accent and all, there is the whole problem of codes. Of all the reminders out there that I'll never be French, this is the main one. I will never be able either to understand or deliver veiled codes. This art of double-talk, which the French have perfected is, for the moment at least, beyond my grasp. For example, you should know that when someone calls you "*cher ami,*" it doesn't necessarily mean "dear friend" and could very likely mean "Drop dead," depending on the intonation of the speaker and his accompanying facial gestures. *À très bientôt*, which literally means "See you very soon," actually means "I

hope we never see each other again," as far as I can figure out. *Ma chère petite dame* (my dear little lady) also
means "Boy, are you a creep." All of this, of course, is
exquisitely polite.

Then there is the use of the word *petit* in general.
Everything, it would seem, is *petit*. I, for example, am
ma petite Harriet, although I am not exactly what you
would call *petite* by any stretch of the imagination. But
unlike *cher, petit* is generally positive, as in a *bon petit
vin* (a nice little wine). Nor are *la petite anglaise* or *la
petite japonaise* pejorative. It would seem that all foreigners are *petit*.

Just as the word *petit* is affectionate, so is the word
grand (big). If someone calls me *ma grande*, for example, it doesn't mean I'm a giant; it means I'm the person's friend. *Vieux* (old) can also be used affectionately,
as in *mon vieux*, or *ma vieille*, but if you say this, it's
best to make sure that the person is in your age group.
If not, it could be insulting.

Being from the Midwest, I'll never get used to the
haughtiness of Parisians or the lack of chitchat. When
my brother, a congenial and friendly fellow, came to
visit me in Paris, I took him to the beautiful Parc de
Bagatelle, not far from my apartment. As we strolled
down the lanes, he would spontaneously say hi to
people. They looked at him as if he had just stripped off
his clothes. I must admit that even after all these years,
my spontaneous midwestern reflex is to smile at strang-

ers. When I forget and do this, the reaction is the same: They look at me like I'm crazy.

Nor will I get used to French friendships, which go beyond the limits we impose upon ourselves in American friendships. A French friend will tell you your lipstick is the wrong color for your dress; she won't hesitate to criticize because you are her friend. The implicit agreement I have with my American friends is quite the contrary: You're my friend, so I do everything in my power to make you feel good, and ignore what is not so good.

When a friend of mine was having some real problems, my husband said to me, "Why are you being so nice to her? Why don't you bawl her out? If she was my friend, I wouldn't let her keep doing those things." I had to explain that if I "bawled out" my friend, I wouldn't have the friend much longer. For him, as for many Frenchmen, you're not a good friend unless you intervene actively in the other person's life. I call this overstepping the boundaries; he calls my type of friendship indifferent and tepid.

Individualism. While it is good that no one looks down on you if you are not a joiner, it is frustrating to realize how deeply the French do not seek, and actively resent, consensus. In the United States, which has gone overboard by persecuting smokers in Salem witch trial-style, once it was decided that smoking was bad, all the good guys jumped on the bandwagon and the smokers were ostracized. In France, even though the government has put its weight behind efforts to get people to quit smoking in public places, the smokers are having none of it. Not only do they not feel guilty; they feel that they are being put upon. Or else, in a somewhat perverse way, they may feel that the law is actually a good thing—for everyone but them. "The government is just doing this to collect money in fines," one unrepentant smoker told me.

Another episode, in which the government called on schoolchildren to bring rice to school to send to Somalia, also drew criticism. Arguments ranged from the obvious (the rice would never get there) to the less obvious (children's innocence shouldn't be exploited for political purposes). Meanwhile, most French kids were dutifully and even graciously giving their rice in an act of solidarity. But it is hard to muster up solidarity in a system that does not encourage links among people. And this absence of links in the form of high school football teams or choirs or theater clubs means that there is very little conviviality in the long run. Another reason I will never be French.

Negativism. The French really are a rather negative lot. Even when things are going well, they find a way to talk about *le mal français* (the French sickness). Many books by Frenchmen have been written on that mysterious subject. One of the reasons I'll never be French is that I am convinced that almost everything is possible if you want it badly enough. My immediate reaction is not "No," but "Yes," or "Why not?" This is definitely not French.

Rules. I'll never be French because I will never get used to the systematic breaking of rules. I think of the butcher shop where I buy meat. Before me in line was a lady with a little white poodle dressed in a red coat. Behind the cashier's stand is a sign that says very clearly, "NOS AMIS LES ANIMAUX SONT INTERDITS" (Our animal friends are forbidden), and in case no one can read, there is a picture of a dog with a big cross painted over it. This, however, does not dissuade people like the lady with the red-coated dog from entering the store. Nor does the owner make a big fuss. After all, rules are made to be broken.

Last but not least, complication . . . and criticism. As a Dane who has been living in France for almost as long as I have remarked, "I have never in my life seen people who can take the simplest thing and make it so complicated." Amen!

As for criticism: "In France, criticism is considered the supreme demonstration of intelligence," wrote high school principal Marc Guiraut. I personally find that too much criticism, or mean criticism, can be stultifying and negative. But then, that is my American point of view.

Okay, so I'm not French and never will be. Even small differences underscore this fact. If I open two windows to create a cross breeze, I am accused of causing a draft. At cocktail parties, I am always backing into plants or the nearest wall because, as an American, I need more space. I still squirm at conversations that take a Rabelaisian turn—and there are plenty of them.

Finally, I'll never be French because, unfortunately, I have never been able to find out the Frenchwoman's secret for looking sexy even when she's standing around in old blue jeans and a T-shirt. Is it because the old jeans are just tight enough without being vulgar and the T-shirt has just the right cut? I remember with awe my friend Chantal, who lived next to me in a maid's room in our student days, as she waltzed up eight flights of stairs in a navy pea jacket she had transformed from a former long coat, with her scarf tied around her hair, just so. She could have stepped out of the pages of *Vogue*.

Not to mention Sandrine, who, although pushing her middle fifties, is the sexiest woman I know. If you manage to dissect what she has on, you still cannot figure out how she arrived at the total effect, and you certainly would *never* ask. So just what is that little *je ne sais quoi* that elevates simplicity into style, an art the French have mastered not just in clothing but in almost every detail of life? After almost twenty years, I'm still trying to figure it out.

So, in spite of the knowledge that I live in France but will never be French, little intrigues like the above, and many, many others, should keep me going for a good while to come. Someday I hope to get it all figured out. And who knows? Maybe I'll even lose my accent along the way. Miracles do happen, *n'est-ce pas?*

About the Author

Harriet Welty Rochefort grew up in Shenandoah, Iowa. A lifelong attraction to France led her to visit Paris during college. In 1971, she hopped on a freighter to Cadiz and ended up in France once again—this time to stay. A freelance journalist, Harriet teaches journalism at the Institut d'Etudes Politiques de Paris. She regularly lectures on Franco-American cultural differences based on *French Toast* and her second book, *French Fried*. Her Web site is www.understandfrance.org.